Jack's Journey USA

One dog's journey to inspire YOUR life of adventure!

By
Dawn Celapino

ISBN-10: 0-692-68962-1

ISBN-13: 978-0-692-68962-2

www.JacksJourneyUSA.com

www.LeashYourFitness.com

www.facebook/leashyourfitness

www.instagram.com/leashyourfitness/

Edited: Arden Moore

Cover Design, Book Interior Design & eBook conversion by manuscript2ebook.com

This book is dedicated to
My Parents, Jack and Norma Celapino
Thank you for watching out for us!

TABLE OF CONTENTS

Foreword

Ah...someday. As in someday, I will get a RV and just travel the back roads. As in someday, I will treat my great dog to a real road trip – the kind with no must-be-there-at-this-time kind of deadlines.

For Dawn Celapino and Jack, her amazing Cairn terrier, someday isn't really in their vocabulary. This pair is more into the now, the today. They are more into leading active lives. And, they are getting the most of each and every day.

We can learn a lot from them. They love to explore new places, hike, swim, paddleboard, and work out together. They get up when the sun peeks above the horizon and leap into a new outdoor adventure.

Remember the late great Charles Kuralt, host of the CBS Sunday Morning Show? He was one of my personal heroes because he got off the main highways, bypassed famous celebrities and took to the back roads and small towns to spotlight ordinary people doing extraordinary things.

Foreword

In a sense, Dawn and Jack are behaving much like Kuralt as you will discover in the pages of this chronicle of the ultimate person-dog cross-country journey. They purposely steered clear of highways whenever they could to motor inside their Spirit RV on local roads, making time to mosey around small towns and have real conversations with people in dozens of states.

I've known Dawn and Jack for more than seven years and can remember the first day I brought my dogs, Chipper and Cleo, to try one of her Leash Your Fitness classes. Her enthusiasm and love for partnering with dogs in a workout are contagious. We would finish each workout class sporting big grins and felt good.

Dawn and Jack serve as ideal role models for all of us who long to stop talking about doing a trip 'someday," and turn talk into action. I think you will enjoy Jack's "side comments" and his obsession with the need to find a body of water to swim in at each stop. You will delight in some of the people Dawn has met at various RV campsites and discover how important family can be to all of us.

Ready for a real adventure with your dog? Call him over and read out loud the adventures of Dawn and Jack on this special journey. They will teach you how to stop thinking about "some day" and how to make each day with your dog a very special one.

Arden Moore, founder of Four Legged Life and
host of the Oh Behave Show on Pet Life Radio

Prologue

Have you ever been somewhere and had a total a-ha moment? You know, one that made you realize that you have to do something besides what you are currently doing? Maybe something BIG and CRAZY?

I had that moment on the top of a mountain in Solvang, CA on March 8, 2014. Jack, my 9-year-old Cairn terrier, and I were on a hike that we had never been on before. It was called Tequepis Trail. It was a really pretty day, not too warm but perfect for hiking. We arrived at the peak of the hike and it was breath taking!

Just picture this - a peaceful lake in front of you. Turn around and there's the Pacific Ocean. The view was so beautiful that I took a video and posted it on our Leash Your Fitness YouTube channel for all to enjoy. I sat on the top of that mountain with Jack and thought, "I want to see beautiful views all over the country with my little guy! Wouldn't it be so awesome to buy a RV and travel with Jack around the country and hike and inspire others to get out and do fun stuff with their dogs?"

As crazy as it sounds, I went home and started looking for a RV! Within a month, I found the perfect one for Jack and me. We named her Spirit because she is a 22-foot Itasca Spirit, but also because we knew that our travel spirits would be on this journey with us.

My mom had recently passed away. It was very sudden, and it had a profound impact on me. I was always one to just jump in and do crazy things. That is how I ended up moving to Maryland when I was 22 years old and to California from Maryland at the age of 27 years old without having a job, a place to live or knowing anyone. It's also how I started my dog fitness business, Leash Your Fitness, by just having an idea. When I get an idea, I go for it. But after my mom passed away, I realized that life is so precious. It can be taken from you at any moment so why put off what you want to do? I knew that this was my time to act.

As I started the planning process, I faced key questions: What would I have to do to drop everything and travel around the country? How could I inspire others to travel and do outdoor activities with their dogs?

Once you commit to doing something, things have a way of falling into place. It started with finding the perfect RV. I looked at one RV and liked it, but it had too many miles logged on the odometer. So, I started looking in the *RV Trader* and online, but nothing really called out to me. I visited all of the RV places in San Diego. When I told them I wanted to spend about $20,000, the sales people laughed and said they didn't have anything in that low price range.

But my luck changed the next week when I attended a RV show being held in a local stadium parking lot. I checked out the models on the first day of the show – most were new and above my $20,000 budget. But then I spotted a RV in the back corner.

"What's the story on this one?" I asked the salesman showing me around. He didn't know. It was just brought in. The second I stepped into this Itasca Spirit, I fell in love. It wasn't too big or too small. It had a great layout and although it was 15 years old, it only had 22,000 miles logged.

The sales guy noticed my keen interest and started pressuring me hard. I started calling everyone that I knew who had a RV to get his or her advice. The salesman put so much pressure on me that I was nearly in tears. I was about to leave when the district manager stopped me and said that if I wanted to put $5,000 down so they would hold it for me. She said she felt confident that they would have no problem selling this RV. So, I got out my credit card and did it.

I drove home feeling confused – everything was happening so fast. I said to God, "Please give me a sign if I am supposed to have this RV or not." Boy did he! That night, I posted on Facebook, "Does anyone know anything about RV's?" My friend, Shawn Velesko, who now lives in Arizona, told me to contact our mutual friend, Jeff Brady, because Jeff now works at La Mesa RV. La Mesa RV just happened to be the RV place selling this particular RV! I hadn't talked to Jeff in 18 years. He was one of my very first roommates when I moved to San Diego, 20 years ago.

I wasn't even friends with him on Facebook, so I messaged him to please call me ASAP regarding a RV. At 7 a.m. the next morning, my phone rings and it was Jeff. He listened to my story about the pushy salesman and even though he agreed that the man used every sales trick in the book, he also said that everything that the man said was true. Jeff just happened to be the salesman who took this RV in on trade so he knew everything about it! The RV was in immaculate shape. The prior owner stored it in a garage and kept meticulous maintenance records. Jeff also said it was rare for La Mesa RV to take in such an old RV, but this one was in such good shape. He said it was a great deal and called me back 20 minutes later to tell me that his boss said that Jeff could handle the sale so I wouldn't have to deal with Mr. Pushy anymore! Things fell in to place so perfectly that I would have been crazy not to buy it. I'm not a religious person, but I am spiritual and I saw the sign – buy this RV and now!

Okay, Challenge 1 was accomplished – the RV was purchased. Next challenge: coming up with a plan to travel the country with Jack and inspire others to get fit with their dog.

Of course, life brings complications. I work part time at a hospital as an x-ray technician. I also own my own business. I am a personal trainer and teach group fitness classes. I'm also the founder of Leash Your Fitness, a company that teaches activities and workout classes for people and their dogs.

Once again, things fell in place. At the hospital, we got a new supervisor who loves to travel. I approached him about my idea of taking a few months off of work. I wasn't sure how he would react and honestly, I was prepared to quit my job if

I wasn't permitted to go.

I was surprised by his response. He told me to go for it, that it was important to travel. "You come back more refreshed," he said.

He checked the work schedule and agreed with one caveat: that I must be back to work by the second week of July. I checked the calendar: this would give me 10 weeks to hit the road with Jack. And as another sign that this journey was meant to be, I could use paid vacation I had compiled and keep my health benefits while on the road!

Third challenge: finding a way to not halt my Leash Your Fitness classes while I was away for 10 weeks. The list of activities include hiking, kayaking, camping, Stand Up Paddle Boarding (SUP), doing yoga and workouts – all with our dogs. When I first came up with the idea to hit the road, I only had one instructor, Naomi Hillery. She was willing to take over my classes, but it would have been a lot for her to handle.

Then out of the blue, one of the gals in class, Crystal Nelson, went back to school for fitness and had the credentials and interest to become a LYF instructor. That took some of the load off of Naomi and gave me the peace of mind, knowing that they would do a good job running the Leash Your Fitness activities while Jack and I were on the road.

And, it gets better. Naomi agreed to complete her Personal Training Certification, so she could help my clients stay fit while I was away.

Challenges #1, #2 and #3 conquered! Now, I could plan my trip. I tried to get some sponsors to offset the expenses of the trip, but many didn't know us and were unwilling to help. Fortunately, a few did see the benefit of this cross-country campaign and came on board as sponsors. Special gratitude goes to:

- **ISLE.** This San Diego company sells surfboards and stand up paddleboards. Jack is an enthusiastic member of the So Cal Surf Dogs and we both enjoy being on the water. Alas, my Spirit RV was not long enough to store a foam surfboard, but the folks at ISLE came up with a solution. They gave us an inflatable standup paddleboard (iSUP) so that we could enjoy the water everywhere we went. The iSUP deflates and fits into a large duffle bag so we could transport it easily. Jack loves to swim – perhaps even more than getting treats – so this iSUP would enable us to enjoy lakes, rivers and other bodies of water at campsites.

- **Kurgo.** This Boston-based company sells dog travel gear. They gave us a life jacket for Jack so he would be safe in the water. Every dog should wear a canine life jacket when doing water sports because it features a handle to enable you to quickly and easily pull your dog out of the water and it keeps your dog buoyant in case he encounters a current or becomes fatigued while paddling. Kurgo also gave us travel essentials, including a dog seatbelt harness, seat cover, travel bowls and hiking booties. They also sponsored our classes throughout the 10-week trek by providing goodies for attendees. They even paid me to teach a few classes in the Northeast. Thank you, Kurgo!

- **One Dog Organic Bakery.** Based in Ohio, this national company makes homemade dog treats. They supplied healthy dog treats for our classes and for Jack. Their treats are homemade, gluten-free and organic – and Jack loves them! Whether traveling with your dog or at home, it is important to feed him quality treats and food.

- **KIND Snacks.** This New York-based company makes meal replacement bars and cereal. They supplied me bags of cereal and with enough bars to get me though the trip. I happily lived on them! They have all kind of savory flavors that were perfect while driving and hiking. We shared them with the class participants and anyone who was KIND to us (which was many people)! It's fun giving people a little "present" when they aren't expecting it!

- **Sun Warrior Protein Powder.** This company gave us enough vegan protein powder to get us through our trip. I bought a little travel blender so I could make refreshing smoothies along the way. We also had sample packets to give to the class participants.

Challenge 4 was complete. Our sponsors helped us get the word out about out our trip, provided giveaways for people we met and defrayed some of the trip's cost.

Leash Your Fitness ranks as one of the first dog fitness businesses in the country. Our success has sparked interest from people around the country who were interested in setting up similar business models. One person to contact us was Paul, the director of a recreation center in Cedar Hill, TX. He was interested in starting Dog Fitness classes at his recreation center. While visiting San Diego, he was unable to observe our class, but agreed to host our first stop in our cross-country trek. In no time, through the contacts that I have, I also booked 10 more classes to teach on our journey. You will learn about each one in the upcoming chapters!

The final challenge: making the RV attract positive attention. My boyfriend, Jim Hahn, owns a sign shop called Clairemont Signs in San Diego that specializes in car wraps. He contacted one of his designers and together, we came up with a design that embodies what this journey was to be all about. We selected yellow – a happy, attention-getting color to be the background color on the RV. Then we added photos on the sides that would depict activities we would be doing on this journey. One image captured Jack and me paddle boarding. Another showed us having fun working out in an outdoor Leash Your Fitness class. There were photos of dog yoga classes, kayaking, group hikes and more. Jack was featured on an Animal Planet show, so we added, "As seen on Animal Planet" to bolster our credibility. And, of course, we posted the names and logos of all our sponsors. And the banner, "JacksJourneyUSA.com" stretched across the RV for all to spot.

The final design meant the most to me. On the front of the RV, we placed a decal of my deceased parents. It was my favorite photo of them – they were holding hands and smiling. I know they were smiling down on us and were very happy for me. My dad was very adventurous and my mom always encouraged me to be independent. I could feel their spirit with each mile on our journey.

Okay, I was all set! I was finally ready to leave San Diego at the end of April and reach Texas in time to teach the first class in early May – before the weather there got too hot. I mapped out the route to make sure Jack and I would be back by July 12 to honor my supervisor's request.

Now it is time for you to join us on this journey. Jack and I hope our journey inspires you to travel and to do fun, memory-making activities with your dog. Ready for a doggone great road trip? Let's begin!

Chapter 1: New Mexico

Tuesday April 28th - *After all of the prep work, we knew it was time to go. We worked on the RV until 11:30 p.m. last night. The last and most important part was getting my mom and dad's photo on there. They will be my travel spirits the entire time. We will be paddle boarding, teaching fitness classes including Dog Yoga, hiking, and trail running all over the country. The RV is bright yellow with JacksJourneyUSA.com on the top so people will know where to follow us. We will be blogging the entire time and posting on our Leash Your Fitness Instagram and Facebook pages. I am very emotional, as I have poured my heart and soul into this journey. All I know is that I am excited about the unknown!*

We pulled out of San Diego at 6 a.m. As I logged my first mile of this emotional journey, I felt the travel spirits of my parents and grateful that the decal of them on the front of the RV would be front and center for all to see and for them to guide me.

I knew that my first day drive was going to be the longest of my journey. I gave myself three days to get to our first official stop, which was in Allen, TX at the home of my friend,

Arden Moore. Day 1 on the road consumed 12 hours of driving with Jack and I stopping for the night in Las Cruces, NM. I countered this long, boring drive by listening to books on tape and podcasts. The best part on the first day was driving through the windmills on Route 10 when leaving California. These big, white windmills are not only beautiful, but also functional as they generate power to the entire valley.

I don't usually like to drive on freeways, but I wanted to get to our first destination as fast as possible. Jack and I stopped a few times to stretch and take a little walk and I'm fortunate that he is an awesome travel partner. He somehow knew when we were in it for a long drive, and he settled in his dog car seat and went to sleep. He woke up every once in a while and looked out the window like a person. I talked to him and told him where we were and what's ahead. The nice part is he never asked, "When are we going to be there?" Twelve hours and 690 miles later, we reached our first campsite off the exit called "Truth or Consequences" in Las Cruces.

When I travel, I usually don't reserve places ahead of time. I never know where I am going to end up, and I sometimes go on detours that take me off of my planned path. This day was no different. I didn't research where we were going to stay, and I was so tired that I just picked the first campground that I saw. It ended up being one of the only RV parks that we would stay in during our journey. The Las Cruces KOA wasn't very crowded. We picked a spot in the back near the tent sites so we could be alone and I let Jack out to run around. He was such a good boy all day. He never whined while in the RV, but he sure was happy to get out and run around.

We organized ourselves, took a walk through the camp and met a few fellow travelers. There was a little dog park in the campground, so I took Jack in to meet the two dogs that were in there. He did not really care about them. Ever since he was little, he has been independent. When he was a puppy, he had a best friend named Biscuit. But when Biscuit and her pet parent moved back to Thailand, Jack and I were both sad. Then Jack made friends with a terrier named Max, but after Max and his pet parent moved, Jack didn't care about any other dog. I suppose he reasoned, "No use making doggy friends. They are just going to disappear." Of course, a dog behaviorist would probably say I am nuts, but I still believe it!

We headed back to camp, planned our next day, made dinner, and went to sleep early! This Day 1 journey brought us into a new time zone – Mountain Time.

Just getting to spend all day, every day, with Jack is going to be so cool. He is my best friend, and I love being with him. When I got Jack, my entire life changed so that I could spend as much time with him as I could. Of course, I started my business because of him, so nobody was surprised when I said I wanted to do a road trip with just him. We have a connection and we understand each other. We are a lot alike. We both like adventure, and we are both very independent. We make a good team!

The next morning I woke up dreading that I had to drive so far again, but I knew we had to do it! I made the executive decision that we were not taking the freeway!

Even though the scenic route was longer, that's the way we were going.

Mommy let me out in the morning to roam around the campsite. There was a big grassy area. Being the adventurous dog that I am, I found the smelliest stuff that I could find, and I rolled around in it. I think it was poop! I was so excited to show mommy what I found that I ran back to the RV. I am not sure why mommy wasn't as excited as I was, but she did start to laugh!

First travel mistake: Don't travel 12 hours in a RV with a full water tank. The weight eats up your gas. I wanted to get rid of some of the water in the tank, so Jack got a bath in the RV on our first day on the journey! He was NOT going to travel all day with poop on him. One thing about Jack is that there is never a dull moment when he is around. He is a 10-year-old Cairn terrier who remains very active and all dog! He is not a prissy dog whatsoever. He loves to do anything that involves water - except get a bath!

There were many reasons for this journey, but a big one was that Jack was 10 years old. I wanted to enjoy as much time with him while he was still active. He possesses lots of spunk, and he is so much fun to be around. I started Leash Your Fitness because of him. I had so much fun exercising with him that I felt that others would feel the same way with their dogs. Jack goes with me on every adventure and has already visited 21 states – and counting. Yes, he has sniffed out waters and performed the "dog paddle" in each of these states.

Chapter 1: New Mexico

The reason that I got a Cairn terrier is that this breed is described as "a big dog in a small body." True to his breed, Jack keeps up with everything that I do. He goes mountain biking with me. He has run 10 miles and hiked over 12 miles in 12,000-foot elevation in Idaho. Cairn terriers are sturdy dogs! That is why the *Animal Planet* crew spent the day with us a few years ago filming a segment for "Mighty Dog" to spotlight all of the activities that Jack does! He is my best friend, and I can't imagine what my life would be like right now if he had never entered it.

After I emptied some water out of the tank, we were off to our first adventure: White Sands National Park. Only a few national parks allow dogs and White Sands was one of them. Time for Jack and me to explore miles and miles of sand dunes! We parked Spirit at a pullover and went exploring. It was so incredible how far you could see white sand. It would be so easy to get lost out there. We were very fortunate to be here in April because the dunes would be too hot for the dogs to explore. The weather was perfect the day we were there. It felt so good to get out and run around after our long day of travel the day before. Jack had a blast running up and down the sand dunes. We were the only ones on the dunes and we felt so free!

When we got back to the RV, a few people stopped to find out about Jack's Journey USA. They got their photos taken with us by the RV. It was so fun to meet them and their dog. We told them how fun it was running around the dunes, so they decided to go explore with their dog. On our first stop, we were already doing what we came to do – inspire others to be active with their dogs!

After we spent time at the White Sands National Park, we were off to Cloudcroft. It was a really cool drive up into the mountains – much better than the freeway! On our way to Cloudcroft, I saw a sign for a hike and decided to investigate. We stopped at a little store to inquire about the hike. The two older men at the counter were very helpful, drawing us a map of where to go if we promised not to tell anyone else about the hike. They didn't want tourists stopping by their little town! The hike was ok but it was getting a little warm for Jack so we didn't make it to the waterfall. It did not feel hot to me at all but Jack does not do well hiking when it is warm outside. I noticed he was panting more than from the start of the hike.

When hiking or spending time in hot weather, it is important to remember that dogs do not sweat like we do. They pant. Dogs perspire through their footpads, which is why it is critical to dip your hot dog in cool water (never ice water – you don't want to unintentionally shock the body) to help him cool off.

Once we reached Cloudcroft, the heat issue disappeared as we discovered little patches of snow! On a short hike to the Mexican Train Trestle, we ventured under a trestle built in the 1890s. According to the Abandoned Trails website, "At the time of its completion, it was the highest standard-gauge track in the world. The line offered both freight and passenger excursion service, often transporting movie stars and other famous guests 6,000 feet upwards into the grand mountains.

58 wooden bridges were constructed, including one "S" bridge (formed by two reverse curves) at a length of 338 feet."

Back at the parking lot, we met the park host and chatted with him for so long that before we knew it, it was 4 p.m.! We would discover that park hosts have interesting stories to share. This particular one studied UFOs and even wrote a book about them. He had a very interesting life and was fun to talk to, but we had to get back on the road! We had a long drive in front of us.

We entered Texas in the dark and it was crazy! The truck drivers fly on the roads. The speed limit is 75 and you had better be going that fast or they would run you over! I was a nervous wreck so I found a truck stop and stayed there for the night. I would much rather drive during the day!

Wednesday, April 29th - *Our first day was full of adventure, just the way we like it! And it is only the beginning!*

Chapter 2: Texas

Besides contending with some crazy truck drivers in Texas, the freeways around Dallas are insane! They interlaced and soared high in the sky, conjuring images of the "space highways" from the 1960s cartoon show, The Jetsons. In that show, futuristic cars flew in the sky. That is what Dallas was like. The looping highways even confused my GPS! I would finally get on the correct road and then my GPS would say, "Go to the light and make a U-turn." Arghhhh! It would definitely take a few days to get used to navigating these highways, but the prime reason I was heading to Big D was to visit my friend, Arden Moore.

Arden had just moved to Allen, a city just north of Dallas, after living 15 years in San Diego County. She was looking forward to seeing Jack and me as we were looking forward to seeing her and her dogs, Chipper and Cleo, and her orange tabby named Casey. Arden is a pet behaviorist, pet first aid/CPR instructor, radio show host, speaker, author and a whole lot more. She is one of the nicest people to know, and I am happy to be friends with her. I remember the first day that she came to my Leash Your Fitness class in 2010. I was so excited to have a "celebrity" in class. We have been good friends ever since.

When my RV parked in front of her house, Arden was there to greet us. And she had a pet posse with her. In addition to her dogs, Chipper and Cleo, she lives with her sister's dogs Jeanne, Maddie and Gracie. Arden and I had a game plan. As soon as Jack and I arrived, we leashed up all SIX dogs and took the "pack" for a brisk walk so they would get used to each other.

Whenever introducing a new dog to your household, it is a good idea to take them to neutral territory to let them get to know each other before allowing them back in the home together.

We both used waist-belt leashes and were able to take all six out together. It was cute seeing all six walking side by side on the wide sidewalks around Arden's new neighborhood.

We have only been gone two days and we are already sleeping in a bed and visiting friends. While Jack hung out with the canine pack inside Arden's home, she took me to dinner to try genuine Texan BBQ. To me, getting to hang out with family and friends in different states ranks much higher on my priority list than seeing tourist attractions on the road. Jim, Jack and I did a cross-country trip four years earlier to visit friends and family all over the country. We were on a mission to reach Pennsylvania in time to celebrate my mom's 80th birthday party. Jack was too big to fly in an airplane cabin and I didn't want him to go in the cargo, so I took a month off and drove from San Diego to Pennsylvania with him in my vehicle. We stayed in dog-friendly hotels but visiting people along the way was what made the trip! When I returned home, I moved from my one-bedroom condo to a three-bedroom one so people could come visit me when they were traveling.

While visiting Arden, I got the privilege to be on her "Oh Behave" show on Pet Life Radio. Arden is a great interviewer. She does her research before each interview, and she is very entertaining. I really enjoy listening to her show so I was thrilled to be on it!

It was nice to spend the morning with Arden. After the radio interview, we took the dogs for a walk around her neighborhood. Twenty minutes into the walk, we spotted a wooded area with a trail. I looked carefully and spotted a creek down the hill. Recent rains in the Dallas area swelled the river so it was deep enough for swimming. Arden had been living here for three months, but had no idea that this creek existed. That's what Jack and I do best: introducing new trails!

We maneuvered the six dogs down to the river. Jack was barking with enthusiasm to let me off his leash so he could swim. Arden's dogs, Chipper and Cleo were also eager to make a splash. As a precaution, we kept Jeanne, Maddie and Gracie on leashes and allowed them to cool their paws along the shore. I can't tell you which dog sported the widest grin by the time we were heading back up to the trail.

Water fun is a major draw for Jack, Chipper and Cleo. All three were among the original members of the So Cal Surf Dogs. This fast-growing sport draws lots of water-loving dogs and plenty of people curious to see how four-leggers ride waves on foam surfboards. In canine surf events, the dogs sport safety vests, balance on the boards and after a little push from their human surf partners, ride the waves into shore. This sport draws local and national television coverage.

Now, I've never been a good surfer, but Jack sure is. He possesses great balance, but he loves to jump off docks and other things to plunge into the water. In fact, he is very good at another canine water sport: dock diving. Fortunately, when he is on a surfboard with Cleo, he stays on the board and doesn't jump off until they reach the shore. We jokingly refer to them as boyfriend and girlfriend. It is sweet to see them so happy whenever they get together – on land, in the water, in San Diego or Texas.

It was a short stay and I was sad to leave, but I was going to get to see Arden again the next day when she came to my first people-dog workout class on Jack's Journey at the Cedar Hill Recreation Center in Cedar Hill, about a 45-minute drive south from Arden's home in Allen.

To reach Cedar Hill that afternoon, Jack and I had to tackle the Dallas freeways again, but this time, I was more mentally prepared and arrived with plenty of time to set up my campsite for the night and meet Paul, our contact from the recreation center. We did a quick tour of the workout location, a nice, large park with plenty of trees for shade, which we would need. The class was set to start the next morning at 7:30 a.m. and trust me, it gets hot quickly in Texas in May.

The campground closest to the park was Cedar Hill State Park. It was a huge park on a lake. When I checked their website before I left there were plenty of sites so I didn't bother making a reservation. I like to arrive and pick my perfect site near the water. Arriving later in the day, the sites on the lake were already taken. We were assigned a decent site across from the lake. I needed a launch area for our SUP, so I quickly made friends with the guy with the killer site right on the lake.

Alex was a super nice guy and Jack and I hung out with him a lot during our stay at Cedar Hill. We even left our iSUP at his site. He had us over for dinner and we let him try our iSUP. We love it when people try new activities and like them. That is one of the reasons we are on this journey is to "inspire people to try new things!"

It was fun watching people walk by Spirit and try to figure out what we were all about. When you have a bright yellow RV with pictures and writing all over it, people stop and take notice. When we were in line at Costco, everyone getting out of their cars would come over and meet Jack. It was so cute, except for the part that we were blocking the gas tanks!

Saturday came and it was time for my first class on Jack's Journey. It is always fun to meet other dogs and other dog parents. It is usually women who bring their dogs to class, but we had a few guys in this class. It is so cute to watch people interact with their dogs. We have every kind of dog come to class from Great Danes to Chihuahuas. We don't dog discriminate and even allow socially aggressive and/ or reactive dogs to class. The dogs are on leash the entire time, and we don't allow them to socialize during class. We keep them focused on the task at hand and not the other dogs. We have found that when they come on a regular basis to a safe environment where they have a job to do, they calm down and are better socially around other dogs. We have had many success stories like this.

As we were setting up the class, I looked up and saw Arden arrive with Chipper, Cleo plus her sister, Deb, friend, Jill and their dogs, Jeanne and Maddie. Arden, Chipper and Cleo took my classes for a few years in San Diego, so I was nice to have a familiar face here in Cedar Hill. And, yes, even Alex from the campsite came, bringing a buddy. That was super cool!

I have been teaching our Leash Your Fitness classes for six years. I am not a dog trainer; I am a personal trainer so my goal for the classes is to give the person a great workout. The benefit to the dogs is that they are with their parents instead of being left at home while their parents work out. The dogs get a mental and physical workout while bonding with their parents. When I started Leash Your Fitness, I didn't know that the dogs would benefit so much from class. It was an added bonus!

Back to the Cedar Hill class. Since I was only going to be teaching in this area for one day, my goal was to show the participants some exercises that they can add to their daily dog walks to make it more of a workout walk. We did some drills in the field, some balance and yoga moves, various exercises on the picnic tables and a little agility to help tire the dogs out more quickly. We also incorporate basic dog obedience in our classes so that the dogs had to "think" during class. This does a few things, it tires the dogs out mentally, and it also requires the parents and the dogs to interact during the class. This makes for a better bonding experience!

The class went well. Everyone went home with a few new exercises to practice and some drills that they could do with their dog. There was a 7-month-old puppy in class and our goal was to tire him out. We succeeded and considered that an accomplishment!

After class, it was time for Jack and I to relax at camp. We were tired after going non-stop for our first 4 days on the road and traveling 1,481 miles. Relaxing wasn't on Jack's agenda, though, so I inflated the iSUP and we went on a 5-mile paddle on the lake. It was a beautiful lake and that was our longest paddle to date.

It went well except for the fact that I let Jack take his Wubba (a Kong water toy), so he was whining non-stop to play with it in the water. At one point, I almost threw it on shore just so I wouldn't have to listen to him whine anymore, but that would have been mean so I just dealt with it. He jumped on and off the SUP for five miles fetching the Wubba and I did my best not to fall off! At one point, he swam to shore and I had to paddle over and coax him back on the board. I am not sure what he thinks about this floating board on the water and what his job is. It is going to take some getting used to.

Mommy is the coolest mommy ever. We are staying next to a big swimming pool! It has to be because there are no waves and the water doesn't taste funny like in San Diego. She even brought me a floating dock so that I could dock dive. This is so much fun!

I am so happy that we were sponsored by ISLE. I would have never thought to bring an inflatable stand up paddleboard (iSUP) on our journey. As so many things happened serendipitously, so did that. A few months before my journey, I went to a beach clean up in San Diego with my friends. ISLE was sponsoring. I was telling a friend about my journey and that I was trying to find a few sponsors. He suggested that I ask the guys at ISLE. After the event, I mentioned it to the marketing guy, Austin. We chatted via email a few times and they were all for me bringing one of their boards. I was so excited! It was one of the highlights of our journey, as you will see. Plus, at our going away party in San Diego, all of my friends tried it. That inspired them to go to ISLE and buy iSUPS while Jack and I were on our journey. We helped sell more than 25 inflatable boards in San Diego plus people all over the country got to try ours.

Back at camp, it is now time to relax. But not really, I am still trying to figure out some things on the RV that needed to be tinkered with. Then Alex showed up with his chair and cooler. He helped me with a few things. One thing is for sure: most people at campsites are good people. That is why I love camping. It is so fun to meet fellow campers.

Alex hung out and we chatted for a few hours. It is always intriguing to meet new people and hear their stories. Alex was going through some confusing times in his life, and I think he just needed a fresh ear to hear him out. I was happy to listen.

Everyone has a story and it is always interesting to learn about them. It is also nice to just be in the present and enjoy someone's company. I think I am going to like this camping stuff!

Chapter 2: Texas

That night there was a beautiful full moon. It was warm and an awesome night to sit by the lake at Alex's trailer and enjoy dinner with him and his friend. They made me fajitas and yummy chocolate chip cookies. It was super nice of them. I was planning on spending the next day there, but found out that a storm was on its way, so we needed to head out ahead of it.

The next morning, I had to make the hard decision not to drive south to Austin, Texas. I really wanted to go there because it sounds like a super cool town and has been voted "Most Dog Friendly City." But Austin was three hours south and in the opposite direction that I needed to go plus there was a storm coming. I decided to leave Cedar Hill early and head to Oklahoma instead. Alex told me about a really cool campground there, so I decided to get there and get a good hike in before the storm hit. Jack and I love to hike and because there had been rain in Texas prior to our stay, all of the trails were flooded. No worries - we just packed everything up and headed to Oklahoma!

Sunday, May 3rd - We have been gone five days and are on our way to our fifth state. We have a full two weeks to do anything that we want. No agenda. No plans. Nobody is expecting us until we have to be in Maryland to teach a class. So let's see where we end up!

Chapter 3: Oklahoma

One thing that I have learned so far on my travels is that Siri (the voice of Apple Products) and my GPS do not always agree. I think Siri has a deal with the gas companies because she gives you some pretty funky directions some times. In this case, she had me going approximately 50 miles out of the way, and she said the road that was the direct route had traffic on it. I am glad that I didn't listen because the drive was super simple and there was hardly anyone on the road. I am not complaining, the first time I did a cross country road trip in 1995, I used AAA books for maps and information so having a GPS and internet access is much easier and faster!

I arrived at Beaver Bend State Park in Oklahoma at 3:15 p.m. It took me two hours to find the perfect camping spot. I am very picky where we camp. I like to be near water, away from other people and in a nice spot. That is why on my blog I always listed the camp site number so other people who want to go to the same campgrounds that I did can just save time and camp where I camped!

The reason it took so long is that this campground was HUGE and spread out on different roads and different loops. The first loop seemed okay until I found out that the river was dam controlled and you weren't allowed to swim in it. That wasn't going to work. Jack can't be near water without swimming. Then I went to the next loop and fell in love with the camp hosts and their dog, a Yorkie-Maltese mix. That dog was the cutest dog ever! They were a super nice couple and I spent 30 minutes chatting with them. I let them know that I might be back because I liked a spot in their loop. I continued to drive and the park continued on an entirely different road. This loop was on a different river that Jack could swim in, plus, it was near the hiking trails. SCORE! So out of courtesy, we drove back to let the nice camp hosts know we wouldn't be staying in their loop so they didn't have to save a site for us. Then we took a drive to the top of the dam, which was the only place in the entire park with cell service.

Because I was supposed to have an "office day" before I left Texas and that never happened, I had to get a little work done on the top of the dam. Not a bad place to have your office. It was the beginning of the month so I had to get my monthly reports done and get my trainers paid. I also had some emails to catch up on and get my blog posted.

I had many nice "office views" on my journey. This view looked over the dam into the canyon below. I sat up there in Spirit and did a little work and made a few phone calls after taking Jack for a little hike around to see the beautiful views. Since this was the only place in the park with cell phone coverage, it was funny how many people were up there doing the same thing!

On the way back to my perfect campsite, we stopped for a hike along the river. It was a raging river on one side of the road and on the other side of the road, men were fishing. It was a huge fishing area and they said the river was even temperature controlled for the fish! I didn't even know that you could do that! I was thinking Jim would have loved it here. He loves to fish. I, on the other hand, do not have the patience to fish and I feel like catch and release is mean to the fish. We usually eat the fish that he catches when we camp together.

On my way back to camp, I was thinking how I didn't do anything that I originally had planned for today. But that is what this adventure is all about, living from day to day and seeing what happens! Speaking of seeing what happens, on my drive back a family of deer walked right out in the road in front of me. It was so cool! It was a great way to end the day!

The reason I like camping in State Parks is because they are usually not as crowded as RV parks. To me they are more relaxing than an RV park with pavement and a lot of amenities that I would never use anyhow. I like being surrounded by the sound of nature and a family of deer roaming in my back yard! Not to mention that State Parks are usually much cheaper than RV parks.

The next day I woke to a symphony of birds. They were singing away. It was so nice to lie in bed and listen to them.

A nice lady stopped by while we were getting ready to go on our hike. She was curious about Jack's Journey. I love it when people stop by to ask about our journey. She gave us a lot of information about the campground and the surrounding area. She was a frequent visitor to the park. It was really nice chatting with her. I told her about the hike that we were planning on doing and she said that maybe she would take her dog on it. Yes! We love to inspire people to get out and enjoy nature and their surroundings. Even if you just take a little nature hike, that is movement that you wouldn't get by just sitting at camp.

We left for our hike at 8 a.m. The Cedar Bluff trailhead was walking distance from camp. We just had to walk down the road and cross a bridge. Of course, we had to stop so Jack could go swimming! You will never meet a dog who loves to swim as much as my dog! It is so fun watching him. His little tail is like a rudder. It moves from side to side when he changes direction, and his little legs are so graceful in the water. He is a super fast swimmer. I can't keep up with him!

There were a few hikes to choose from so I chose the longest one, Skyline Trail. I am not the best at directions so it was a little confusing as they all intersected at one point. I ended up back on the trail that I started on which wasn't a bad thing because there was a super cool view of the river. There was also cell coverage there so I posted a photo on our Facebook page to share what we were experiencing with our friends.

We have been posting photos to our Leash Your Fitness Facebook and Instagram pages as well as blogging on our Jack's Journey USA website. We have a following and building the number of people enjoying our adventure. Jack is such a "camera hound," so I get some really cool photos of him and people love that! It helps that he is so darn cute!

My goal was to do part of the Skyline trail and then turn around, but the trail was so beautiful that we ended up doing the entire hike. The birds were singing. The trail was completely shaded. There was a nice mixture of ascents and descents, and there were water spots where Jack could swim. It was the perfect hike and one of my favorite on the entire journey. Because I had hiked the other trail the day before, I figured that if I kept going on this one, it would bring me out near there and I could just walk the road home. I took a chance and went for it!

We didn't see another person the entire hike! We followed the signs the entire way. The trail was really well marked which was good because I have a tendency to get lost, as I already mentioned! A few times, the trail crossed the creek, which was a little confusing, but I was so proud of myself for not getting lost. Jack was having the time of his life chasing squirrels, swimming and hanging with his mom. He has a really good recall so he mostly hikes off leash unless we are on a crowded trail or we come to another dog or animal. He just loves to run around free, and I think it is important to let dogs be dogs and let them run around as long as it is safe.

For the most part, Jack stays on the trail with me. When I think there may be something up ahead, I have him trained to stay behind me. He won't even go in the water until I say it is okay. Some rivers are too swift to swim in, and are not safe. I have spent a lot of time training Jack and for the most part, he is a really good boy.

I have noticed that often the mileage on trail maps are not entirely accurate. According to the sign at the beginning of the trail, the Skyline trail was supposed to be seven miles. I use the free app, Map My Run, on my phone to track where I am and how far I have gone. Even when there is no cell coverage, the GPS usually works. After nine miles, I was getting a little nervous as to why we weren't approaching the end. I could hear the raging river that I hiked along yesterday so I knew we must be getting close. We came to the area where we were yesterday and then started walking up the road. I wasn't entirely sure how far it was going to be but it was a beautiful day and we were enjoying every minute of it!

The hike ended up being 12 miles. It was an epic hike. There were a few steep hills, stairs and it was long but we took in every bird, butterfly, beautiful tree and water hole. It was a great day, and I felt blessed to have beautiful weather to enjoy!

Jack passed out when we got back to camp. I, on the other hand, had to get some work done. I was trying to keep up on my blog posts and keep my photos organized. I am weird like that. They will all be in separate folders for each location and easy to find when I get home. Back in the day when there was film, I would develop my film and have my photos in albums by the time I got home from vacation. I love my photos and they are wonderful reminders of all of the fun that we have!

If you want to see any of the photos or get more information on any of our stops, head over to the JacksJourneyUSA.com blog and follow along!

Chapter 3: Oklahoma

After Jack rested, we headed over to the playground where I did some yoga stretches and a few upper body exercises. While working out, a family of deer walked right past us! It was so beautiful! Much better view than any gym I have been to!

I then took Jack to the river to let him swim a little. The cold water does his legs good after a long hike. We were both ready for a good night sleep. The storm was heading our way so tomorrow's plan depends on the weather.

I woke to a very cloudy day so we packed up and drove to a little hike to see if the rain was going to come or not. This hike was a strange one. It was called, Lookout Mountain Trail so I was a little confused when then trail went down. I never did see a lookout but it was fun to get out and do another hike. The rain never came and I really wanted to take Jack kayaking on the river. I decided to chance it, and we went for it. The guys at the Kayak outfitter were funny. They weren't concerned about the storm. They said you can't go by the weather because it changes all of the time, and they encouraged us to go. I was so happy that we did!

We were the only ones on the river besides a few fishermen. It was so peaceful. For 90 minutes, I took my time paddling and just enjoyed the scenery. I was so happy that for once, Jack didn't even want to go swimming. The water was 48 degrees, so he would have been shivering and miserable. He just lounged in the front and took in the views. We could see the trail that we hiked yesterday, and we watched some deer scale the hillside.

It was a glorious end to a fabulous find. Thanks to Alex at our last stop for recommending this campground!

We headed into Broken Bow, and I found a coffee shop that had WiFi. I bought a salad in exchange for the WiFi code. I had to get some work done that required the Internet. I sat inside Spirit for a few hours working. It was so fun chatting with all of the people who stopped to see what Jack's Journey USA was all about. One lady came because her mother was there and called her to tell her about us. She dropped everything that she was doing and brought her kids to meet Jack, who unleashed his canine charm.

I had to get on the road because I don't like driving at night. We were on our way to Arkansas. There were a lot of campgrounds to pick from in Hot Springs, so I found one outside of the city on a lake with hiking trails. Do you see the pattern here? Still, it is always a mystery as to what we will find at the next stop. And as usual, we weren't disappointed!

Chapter 4: Arkansas

It is always funny finding campgrounds. We exit the freeway and go on so many back roads that we have no idea where we are going to end up. It was dark when we arrived at Lake Catherine State Park. The park host was so nice. He came out and helped us back into a site. I couldn't see anything so I just picked any site for the night. The bugs were so bad! It was crazy. They were so small that they could get through the screens. Good thing that we had electric as I closed all of the windows and turned on the air conditioning because it was still 85 degrees outside. I was worried that this was going to be a problem here but the strange thing was, that was the only problem I had with bugs during the entire stay.

We woke up the next morning to a beautiful day with a beautiful lake across the road. We love it when that happens! I wasn't sure how hot it was going to get so we left for a hike as soon as we woke.

The hiking trails were at the end of the campground. They were really well marked. There were three to pick from, and they were all color-coded. A half-mile into the trail, a waterfall came into view. It was so beautiful. I sat and enjoyed it while Jack swam and jumped off rocks into the pool beneath it. I was thinking that this would be a good place to bring my beach chair and hang out and read while Jack enjoyed swimming. I love waterfalls and Jack loves to swim so this was perfect!

We headed up the trail. I felt like I was in the rain forest. The trees and vegetation that were surrounding the trail were so lush. I approached the top of the trail to find a vista of the lake. I just sat there and thanked God for this experience. I feel so fortunate to be on this journey with my best friend. Jack has been such a great travel companion. He is as excited as I am at each new adventure. I am finding the coolest spots that have ample opportunity for us to explore and be adventurous. That is what we love the most. Jack is a super active dog, and it is so fun to watch him enjoy the things that he loves to do! It makes me so happy.

After we finished the hike, we walked through the park, and it was super cool. Plenty of lakeside campsites were available and one even had a dock. Jack loves to dock dive so I was hoping that we could get that site for the rest of our stay! This journey is all about Jack. Good thing I like water as much as he does!

Each campground has different rules and at this one, you had to physically go to the office to pay for your site. I don't understand why they can't take a credit card over the phone but rules are rules. So we drove up to the office and paid for site number 42, the one with the dock. The site was fantastic! Jack was super excited! Instead of taking my chair to the waterfall, I took it to the dock, and Jack dock dived the rest of the afternoon. We had many park visitors stop and take photos of him. It is a sight to see my little guy jumping off the side of the dock into the water. He loves it!

In the sport of dock diving, dogs run down a dock and jump into a long pool of water that is marked off on the sides with measurements. Judges decide the distance each dog jumps in the air before splashing into the pool. There are different categories of dogs. There are not many dogs as small as Jack, so he usually wins in his category every time we enter a competition. Dock dogs get so excited and it is very loud with all of the barking going on. It is just another fun activity to do with your dog.

One of the people who stopped by to chat with us was a gal named Shelley Mules. She caught my attention because she was walking two beautiful black labs. I asked her about her dogs, and she proceeded to tell me how she found them in Texas. It was a crazy story so I asked her to return later and I would do an entire blog post about her.

It was a good thing that we had Internet and cell coverage at this spot. I had another radio interview to do, this time with Kelli Corasanti and her "It Just Takes One" show. Kelli is my business coach and a good friend and mentor. I will be stopping to see her later in my journey. She did a super informative interview with me. Kelli was one of the first people to hear about my idea of Jack's Journey. When

I returned from my trip to Solvang and had this crazy idea, Kelli gave me the courage to go for it! She had me write down my plan, come up with ideas on how to execute it and mainly she believed in my idea. Without her guidance, it may still be just an idea. It is good to have people who believe in you and inspire you to try new things and go for your dreams! I look forward to my visit with her.

This campsite was so perfect. It even had a little workout area. I brought my TRX suspension device with me. A Navy Seal developed it so that the troops could work out while they were on deployment. You can hang it from anywhere and do every exercise imaginable with it. I do all of my workouts outside in San Diego for myself and with my clients. We have beautiful parks and beautiful weather so why not? I took all of my workouts outside when I got Jack because I never wanted to leave him when I worked out. I haven't been back to a gym since. I used the TRX in Oklahoma in the playground when deer were walking by and now I am using it lakeside to workout. I love my gyms on this trip! There was even a hook at the campsite that worked perfectly! I found out later that the hook was really for a lantern.

After my workout and dinner, Shelley and her dogs stopped by. It was so fun chatting with her. She had a really unique story. She was traveling with her three large dogs in a 37-foot RV pulling a 20-foot trailer with a SUV on it. I thought I was brave taking off in my 22-foot RV alone with one dog. She definitely outdid me!

Shelley was from Wisconsin and travelled to Texas. That is where she found seven black labs on a property that a hoarder lived on. She saw them because two of the labs got under the fence that separated her place of stay and the engineers. Her dog went to see what was going on and meet the pups. The puppies were about 14 weeks old. She could tell right away that the dogs were feral and not used to people. It took several weeks of feeding them treats to get them to trust her, but eventually they did and she captured all seven pups. The sad part was that the owner didn't even care! It was a series of crazy events but she finally got most of the dogs adopted out except for two and they were traveling with her along with her three rescue dogs.

It was a really nice night on the water and thank goodness all of those pesky bugs weren't around. Shelley and I chatted until after dark. It was so much fun chatting with a fellow traveler. Jack went in the RV to sleep because we had a long day, and he isn't much for playing with puppies.

The next morning, we woke up to a beautiful sunrise. The lake was calm so we got out the iSUP and went on a paddleboard journey around the lake. It seemed that we were the only ones awake. It was so quiet. Jack was a good boy for most of the tour, but he couldn't take it anymore. He really wanted to go swimming. Since we got the lake front site, we never went back to the waterfall yesterday so we paddled there and Jack got to swim while I enjoyed looking at the waterfall. I can't think of a better way to start the day.

We headed back to camp and had breakfast and Jack was so excited to go dock diving again. He ran down to the dock and stood there staring at me until I went down and let him have his fun. I decided to go swimming while he jumped in time and time again! I relaxed on the dock with my chair and book while throwing Jack's Wubba what seemed like 300 times. It is nice to be at the campgrounds before the tourists start arriving. We like our alone time and we had plenty of it since the campground, lake and hiking trails were practically vacant.

Jack finally took a break from swimming so we took a walk up to see Shelley and her RV. She and her five dogs were leaving soon. We just had to see for ourselves what she was driving with all of those dogs! OMG! There it was: a 37-foot 1990 RV with a 20-foot trailer with a SUV on it. Wow! Shelley had her hands full with all of those dogs. But I know she is up to the challenge in navigating with these dogs. It is my wish that the two labs get adopted into loving, homes because they are so sweet and nice.

We bid goodbye, wished them a safe journey and headed back to camp. I plan to stay in touch with Shelley on Facebook. I got some work done and sat and read while Jack rested before our hike. We have one more hike to do before we leave tomorrow. Sprinkles of rain began to fall and the sky started to become cloudy. But this was mild weather and I am grateful that we have been ahead of tornados and heavy rain that hit Texas and Oklahoma after we left those states.

I woke up the next morning to a light sprinkling of rain and no voice! I started to get hoarse yesterday but today it was worse. Thank goodness my radio interview was yesterday and not today! I hardly ever get sick so not sure what this is all about. It may be due to the all of the different plants and vegetation I have been around. We went for one last walk around the park and I let Jack dock dive a few more times before leaving. It is hard to leave this perfect campsite but we are off to see my cousin, Nancy, in Hernando, Mississippi, which is south of Memphis. It's hard to believe we are heading to our eight state in just 11 days.

I was so sad to leave this campsite. I just stood on the dock and looked at mommy like "why do we have to leave?" I wanted to move here! We have everything that we need. Water, a dock and beautiful hiking trails. I just didn't understand why we had to move already?

Chapter 5: Mississippi

As we near Memphis on the way to Hernando, the drive was uneventful until we neared Memphis. This Tennessee city was full of heavy traffic and far-too-much construction work on the roadways. I really dislike traveling through cities, but sometimes you have to do it. Plus, I wanted to show Jack where his namesake, my dad, came down the Mississippi River in a canoe when he was 70. I believe I get my sense of adventure from my dad. He was 77 years old when he passed away from lung cancer in 2005, the same year Jack, my dog, was born. I wanted to get a dog for a long time but I knew it wasn't the right time. I was traveling back and forth to Pennsylvania often to see my dad because he was sick.

Dad passed away on February 22, 2005 and my dog was born on February 5, 17 days earlier. I went through a very bad time after my dad passed away. I became depressed and gained a lot of weight. I had been researching dog breeds and realized that the Cairn terrier was a perfect breed for me. I was an avid mountain biker at the time, loved to camp and be active. I lived in a one-bedroom condo and I am a proud "neat freak," so I didn't want a hairy, shedding dog. I grew up with

Rottweilers and German Shepherds, but knew that a smaller dog would be a better match for me. The Cairn terrier fit all of my needs and wants.

I reached out to a breeder who placed an ad in the newspaper about a litter of Cairn terriers. Before you knew it, I had adopted one of her puppies. When the lady asked me what I was going to name him, I had no clue. I hadn't even thought of it just like I hadn't thought of buying any dog supplies! But my dad was on my mind and just like that, I knew that I would name this pup Jack in honor of my dad.

I didn't know about puppy mills or shelter dogs at the time or crate training or even owning an inside dog. I am from Pennsylvania and always had 'outside' dogs. Heck, I don't even remember ever having a leash! But nowadays, dogs are much more part of the family and I learned a lot about raising a puppy and trust me, there were definitely some trying times during Jack's first year. I thought crate training sounded cruel so I didn't do it. That was my first mistake. I came home far too many days to find poop all over the patio. In addition, Jack also had severe separation anxiety because I took him with me everywhere. I was going to college at the time and I would sneak him into the classroom in my backpack! I fell in love with him and he took over my life.

He was very shy so for the first few years that he didn't allow anyone else to pet him. He was always around people and other dogs, but was always very aloof – except with me. To this day, we call him the Fun Police because when other dogs are playing, he runs over and barks at them to settle down. He entertains himself and does not rely on anyone else (except for me!).

When I got him, I was doing corporate fitness trainings and would sneak him into my jobs. When they started figuring it out, they would tell me that I couldn't bring him. One by one, I quit every job that I had so I could be with Jack. I moved all of my workouts, as well as my clients' workouts, outside. I saw how much fun I had with Jack so I started incorporating my clients' dogs into their workouts and they loved it. That is how my company, Leash Your Fitness, was eventually born. Yes, Jack has had a major impact on my life, and I would not change any of it!

Okay, back on the road. We pull into the driveway of Nancy's house in Hernando, MS just as my cousin was getting ready to pick up her 7-year-old son, Carson, from school. So, we decided to pick him up in Spirit. It was so cute to see his face as he walked out of the school to find his mommy in a big yellow RV with photos of Jack all over it. The teachers got a kick out of it as well! Carson was so excited to ride in the RV that he couldn't wipe the grin off of his face for hours.

By the time that I got to Nancy's house, I had no voice at all! I felt bad because I hadn't seen her in a long time and was looking forward to catching up. She likes to talk, so I just listened as she showed me around her beautiful house and introduced Jack and me to her three cats. Jack was not sure what to think! He loves to chase kitties. Well, most cats. It depends on how they react to him. At Arden's house, her cat, Casey, is confident and lives with five dogs, so he didn't give off any fear vibe that would trigger a chase from Jack.

Inside Nancy's house, there were three cats staring back at Jack. One bold feline came right up to Jack, and it was as if she told him, "Listen, Mister, this is my house so don't even think about messing with me!" Jack heeded her warning and then turned his attention toward the second cat who had less moxie and ran into another room.

Nancy showed me to my room and there was a lump in the bed. Underneath the covers was the third cat! It was too funny. This cat hid out of sight during our entire visit.

As for Jack, he loved being at Nancy's house. It was probably lucky for us that it was too early in the season for her pool to be open or else he would have been obsessed with it. She had a huge back yard that backed up to a large patch of trees. Jack had a blast running around and exploring.

What is wrong with all of these kitties? Don't they know that they are supposed to allow me to chase them? That is part of the fun. I am going to have to keep searching for a kitty who is afraid of me. I know that I will find one on our journey sooner or later! Now, I don't plan to hurt any cats, but I sure love chasing them!

It was nice being in a house after being on the road for 11 days. Sure, I love being in the RV, but Nancy's house is roomy and features a large shower. The shower in the RV works great, but it is tiny. Plus, I was able to wash the sheets and my clothes. Camping is dirty!

While at Nancy's house, a storm erupted. I had parked my RV in her driveway on a slight angle and the heavy, strong rain caused a leak in the overhead bed. After the rain stopped, Nancy's husband, Bill, helped me to figure out where the leak was coming from. We took the garden house and sprayed water on the top of the RV and over all of the windows. We finally found the area that was the problem and I used the caulking that I brought with me to fill in any gaps. What we were not able to figure out was why the floor under the mat on the driver's side was wet. It remains an unsolved mystery. Of course, Jack just liked the hose part while we were treating the leak, so we sprayed him much to his delight. This dog loves anything water as long as there is no soap involved!

While we had the hose out, we gave Spirit a bath. She was looking a little sad so we freshened her up and gave the inside a good scrubbing, too. When you live in such a small space, it is nice to keep things neat and clean. Plus, Nancy is a clean freak like me, so she was in her glory helping me!

That afternoon I had a Skype call with a gal from Amsterdam who wants to start people-dog fitness classes similar to mine. I was glad my voice came back for the call! I do consultations like this with people from all over the world that want to get classes started. It was so cool speaking to someone from another country and hearing the differences in culture. She was attempting to teach her classes with the dogs off leash. I tried that when I first started my business, but it didn't work for obvious reasons. That is why I called my business "Leash Your Fitness" – not "Unleash Your Fitness." When I explained to her how the classes run smoother when the dogs are under control and on leash, it made sense to her. She was a little concerned because in Amsterdam most dogs are off leash most of the time, unlike in the United States where people are used to having their dogs on leash at all times. I was excited for her to get her classes going and follow her progress on Facebook.

 If your dog is trained, trusts you and is in a safe environment, there is no reason you can't have him off leash. Unfortunately, all dogs aren't trained and they all have different backgrounds and temperaments, so to make the class setting safer and in control, I made the leash rule mandatory to keep everyone safe and on equal ground.

After the call, Nancy, Jack and I spent the day running errands. I had to stock up on groceries and get a few items for the RV. The temperature was mild, so Jack was fine waiting in the car as we ran in and out of stores. He is so attached to me that I was afraid to leave him at Nancy's by himself. I never know what he is going to do, and it usually ends in something getting torn to shreds. He has never gotten over his separation anxiety, and I am afraid this trip is going to make it worse since we are together all day, every day. I harnessed him inside Nancy's car and did not take a long time to finish our errands. He was a good boy and happy to be with us.

Bill grilled steak and made a delicious salad for us that night. Why do salads always taste so much better when other people make them? I have to admit that cooking is not my strength, and I eat pretty simply while on the road. I stock up on lots of vegetables and hummus, fruit, nuts and canned chicken, black beans and lots of KIND bars! The only real meals that I ate on the road was a salad in Broken Bow and, of course, the Texas BBQ place that Arden took me to in Allen, Texas.

Chapter 5: Mississippi

Nancy and I played a couple of games of Gin during my visit. Her mom – my Aunt Dorrie – and my mom were best friends growing up. Nancy and I are much younger than our siblings, so we spent a lot of time together when we were young. We spent many summers camping together in my family's travel trailer. Our moms loved playing cards so for old times sake, we played a few games in their honor. It was fun reminiscing about the old days.

We are both orphans now. Our parents and grandparents are all deceased. It is really sad to think about. Thank goodness that we have such fond memories of growing up together. I remember that we would call each other every Christmas morning and compare what we got for Christmas. It was the year that she got the rocking chair so she could rock her newborn that I realized that our lives were taking different directions. That was over 20 years ago. Our lives took very different turns, but we still keep in touch and chat often.

The next morning, Jack woke me up with a bout of reverse sneezing. I am wondering if the pollen is getting to both of us. He was okay after his little episode, but I still had no voice! I am glad that it came back a little yesterday for my Skype call but now it was gone again! While Nancy and I had our coffee, Jack ran around outside. When he returned, we picked 15 ticks off of him! I was mortified. He is on the tick medicine Revolution, but I guess it doesn't work here! Nancy was an expert at finding them as she finds them on her cat. I always say Jack is a tick magnet but this was ridiculous. No more roaming for him!

We decided that it would be best to leave on a Sunday instead of driving through Memphis and Nashville traffic during Monday morning rush hour traffic. I really hated to leave so quickly. I probably should have planned that better, but we had a nice two-day visit.

Reverse sneezing in dogs may be caused by sinus irritation. It is sounds like exaggerated and rapid inhalations through the nose and may sound like snorting. It usually only lasts for a minute or two. When I gently scratch Jack's neck, the sneezing subsides.

I looked on a map and found a green area with water so that is where we headed next. Not very scientific but those are the two things that we like to do, hike and swim. We had no idea if there would be a campsite or what the campground would be like, but as usual, we took our chances and it paid off!

Chapter 6: Tennessee

I am finding that the secret to travel is to travel on Sunday. There is little to no traffic and thankfully, no construction. When we reached Knoxville, we entered Central Standard Time. After many boring miles on freeways, we exited and drove on a bunch of back roads and even through a few neighborhoods. I had no idea where we were going to end up and all of a sudden, there was a huge dam! I should have known we were getting closer when we passed the Dam Store! Yes, that IS it's name. When we reached Douglas Dam Campground, it was 7 p.m. I looked at the RV's odometer: we have now traveled 2,536 miles so far on Jack's Journey.

At the campground's entrance, there was a kiosk that displayed a layout of the park. As I studied it to figure out where to set up camp, people approached and inquired about Jack's Journey. I thought that they may be camp hosts because park hosts are usually at the entrance to the park, but they informed me that the park host was riding in his golf cart around the park.

Almost on cue, the park host pulled up on his golf cart. He was kind of grumpy. I asked if there were any available sites and his reply was, "Yep." So I asked if there were any sites on the water and his reply was, "Maybe." He proceeded to draw me a little map of where to go. Just as I was wondering why he just didn't lead me there in his golf cart, he finally said, "Just follow me." He took me to the most beautiful spot in the entire campground. It was overlooking the majestic lake. The site had plenty of grass for Jack to play in and there was an easy lake access. We were so happy AGAIN! I had to back down a steep gravel hill with a bend in it to park Spirit. The grumpy park host watched from the road. After I parked Spirit perfectly he declared, "Pretty good for a girl!" It meant the world to me to get a compliment from him. I responded by giving him a big hug and thanking him for steering us to this perfect spot.

We met many friendly people at this park, including six camp hosts. We became friends with all of them (except Mr. Grumpy. We never saw him again). One of the park hosts was Mr. Grumpy's wife. She stopped by to ask me to put Jack on a leash because he was running around in the grass by our RV. She ended up staying and chatting with me for an hour. I never did put Jack on a leash because he just stayed hanging out with us at the camp. I told her that I gave her husband a hug and her response was, "Good, he needs one!" She was super nice – a nice compliment to Mr. Grumpy.

We also became friends with our neighbors, Susan and Sonny, who have been traveling for 14 years. She used to be a professional truck driver and now she and her husband just live on the road. Their business card says "Professional Bums" so they gave me a lot of resources and advice for my future travel. I shared some of their recommended resources in the back of the book.

Chapter 6: Tennessee

Mommy lets me run around and play because she knows that I won't go anywhere. Why would I? I have a pretty good life with her. We do all kinds of fun things together. Plus, I know I will be in BIG trouble if I run off and I don't like to make mommy mad. I didn't even roll around in any of the dead fish that were by the lake even though they were very tempting!

There was one little hike through the trees at the park that was relatively flat. Jack and I ran that section and then walked the entire park. There were three sections to this park and we got the best part and definitely the best campsite! Once again, our campsite angels were with us! While walking the park, we stopped and chatted with many of the campers. We love to meet new people and most people want to know what we are doing. Our RV is definitely a great conversational icebreaker! We met a nurse and her husband who sold everything they owned and now live in their RV and work as camp hosts. They fell in love with Jack. It turns out that the husband is very talented at woodcarving. He took a few photos of Jack and promised to do a carving of him. Before we left the campground, his wife told me that he was researching Cairn terriers because he thought Jack was such a cool dog.

I get told that a lot. Jack is a cool dog, and he listens really well. People think that he was born that way but as most dogs, he wasn't. I have spent a lot of time training him. When I was researching his breed, I was told that Cairn terriers are hard to train because they are so independent. When he was a puppy, I took him to a six-week puppy training class, but by the time that we went, he already knew most of the commands that we learned in class. Still, it was good for socializing and I am glad that we went. I think it is important if you are going to have a dog to have a well-behaved one so that he is welcome everywhere.

I have been around dogs all of my life. When I was young, they used to do the dog training classes in our large back yard in Pennsylvania, and I would watch them. My dog prior to Jack was also a super good Rottweiler named Addy. She was more of a lap dog than Jack is, and she also went everywhere with me. My insurance guy at the time back in the 1990's, thought that I was crazy when I bought a new car so that Addy could see out the window easier. If you are going to have a dog, it is worth it to take the time to train him. Dogs are happier when they have direction, have jobs to do and are made to think.

The best part about Douglas Dam Park was the stand up paddle boarding (SUP) that we did. Have I told you lately how much we love our iSUP? We highly encouraged other travelers to purchase one because we have explored so many cool places that we would have never seen without being on the water. I use my app called Map My Run on my phone to see how far that we paddle. I keep it in a waterproof case that goes around my neck. We paddled three miles one day up the coast of the lake. It was fun seeing all kinds of beautiful homes and a campground with a big bouncy thing on the water. Another day, we paddled 2.5 miles round trip to an incredible island that was fun to explore.

The water was warm here, and Jack and I both swam a lot! This is the first time that I actually swam with Jack. Usually, he just stands on the shore when I swim. I think he trusts me more and more. It was fun to swim with him.

I threw his toy and we raced to it. If I won, then I threw it further so he had to swim more. Jack is a really strong and fast swimmer so it is wonderful to race with him.

Swimming is such good exercise for both people and dogs. This low-impact activity helps the joints, and it also works every muscle. If you swim fast enough, you even get your heart rate elevated!

The best part was when I got to show our new friends how to SUP! We were talking to Susan and Sonny in the morning before we took off on our paddle. They were telling us how the other camp hosts had just returned from Hawaii, and they really wanted to get a SUP. We asked her if she wanted to try it and to let the other hosts know that they could try it, too. When we returned from our paddle, everyone was on shore in bathing suits ready. Susan didn't think she would be able to stand up on it but she did! Jack even joined her on one of her tries. The hosts from Hawaii loved it as well. They said that they were definitely going to buy one! It made me so happy to introduce a new activity to our new friends.

We were so sad to leave this campground, but that seems to be a theme everywhere we go. We formed some great friendships and this site was so beautiful and perfect. We weren't sure where to go because I really wanted to go to Ashville, North Carolina, but once again it was in the wrong direction. Susan sat down with me and went over our options for our next stop on the way to Annapolis, Maryland where we are going to teach our next class. We're heading northeast and she did not steer me wrong !

Chapter 7: Virginia

Jack has added three states to his travels: Tennessee, Mississippi and Virginia! The drive from Douglas Dam to Hungry Mother State Park was the easiest and quickest so far! We didn't want a long drive since we enjoyed the morning SUPing at Douglas Dam with our new friends, plus we had to stop and get food. It has been two weeks since we left San Diego and this is our first stop for food. I stocked us up well before we left because I was not sure if I would be able to find my favorite foods on the route. There are many benefits to traveling in a RV, including always having a bathroom, bed and food with you. Those three come in handy!

We arrived in Marion, Virginia home of Hungry Mother State Park around 5:30 p.m. We had traveled 2,536 miles in two weeks. We knew we were no longer in California when we spotted a tractor at the stoplight next to a motorcycle. There are so many joys in traveling to new areas!

We stopped at the office to inquire about campsites, but they weren't open so we just explored the park until we found the perfect site! There were three separate campgrounds to choose from. We met a local man outside the office who was curious about Jack's Journey. He said he was counting down the days until his kids were out of school and he could start traveling more. He loved the idea of taking his dog and didn't know that you could take them to so many places. That is what we are here for – to let people know all of the great things to do with your dog! I told him about all of the beautiful campsites on the water we have visited. He told us that we probably wouldn't find a site on water at this campsite. I guess he underestimated us!

Once again, we found another beautiful spot at this campground. It was next to a bridge and a creek. Jack was out of the RV and in the water in no time! There were ducks swimming right next to him. It was so cute. One kept quacking at him, but he just ignored her and she swam away. Jack doesn't chase ducks when he is swimming, which is a good thing.

The camp hosts weren't home so we set up camp and took a 2-mile walk on the Lake Trail. It sure was pretty there! There were lots of trees surrounding a beautiful lake.

The camp hosts came home and let me know that we had to go up to the office to pay. I guess there was another office that I hadn't seen. It was once again a strange rule regarding payment. I was not sure why you couldn't pay the camp hosts. I had already hooked up the water and electric and wasn't about to unhook everything and drive up there so I told them I would run up there tomorrow and pay since it was nearly closing time. Before I knew it, the lady camp host was back, and she took us for a ride in their golf cart up the office to pay.

She gave us a tour of the campground. There were a lot of amenities, which is why it was voted best campground in Virginia in 2014 and the most expensive one we had stayed at so far! It was supposed to be $40 per night for non-residents of Virginia, but they only charged us $30, which was fine by me. We paid for our usual two nights. We found that was about our limit at each campsite. We usually did everything there was to do and moved on.

The camp hosts were really nice. I was teasing her when she brought me back that I would be over for dinner. She said they had already eaten but I could come over tomorrow. I didn't go over for dinner the next day, but they came over to visit with Jack and I and to see if we wanted to go for a walk with them.

We slept great but it was COLD in the morning! We left for our hike, and it was only 54 degrees, but it felt much colder. I didn't dress warm enough so I walked really fast! The hike was mostly uphill so that helped. We started from our campsite to the Lake Trail and then we went straight UP on the Molly's Knob trail. The trails were well marked and were ideal for biking and running. The view at the top was breathtaking, and we spent some time up there being thankful for our journey so far. We feel so blessed with the friendly people that we have met, the beautiful weather we have had and the amazing campsites where we have stayed! We are trying to give back at each place that we stay and pay it forward, even if it is just giving our neighbor a KIND bar, a bag of One Dog Organic treats or a Kurgo collapsible pet bowl.

The hike ended up being 8.5 miles because we added on the CCC trail on the way back. It was a pretty easy trail and we got a great view of the river. It was torture for Jack, but I wouldn't let him go swimming because he had a bellyache from all of the swimming that he had been doing. The river was also a little fast for him. He doesn't get his way all of the time!

We got back to camp in time for lunch and to RELAX!! It was a perfect day for it. I finally got to read my book, wrote a few blogs posts and chatted with the neighbors. They were here for a volleyball tournament. The park had a large sand volleyball area, a huge playground, a restaurant, gazebo for weddings and other events, laundry room and all kinds of water sports. They also held races here like mountain bike and road races. It was early in the season and a weekday so most of that was not happening. Instead, we were able to enjoy the place with few visitors just the way we like it.

I am still having a hard time with the "relaxing" time so I also pulled out the TRX and got a little workout in next to the creek. Another beautiful workout spot! Once again there was a lantern pole that was perfect for my TRX suspension trainer. The camp host thought that was great that I was working out on the lantern pole!

When the camp hosts had stopped by, they informed us that there is free WiFi here. That was a first. Most of the campgrounds that we had stayed at so far did not have WiFi but had cell coverage. I have been able to use my iPad and phone to answer emails and get a little work done. With WiFi I could post my blogs, write my newsletter and get all of the classes scheduled back in San Diego. It is awesome to be able to get things done on the road. Although, I feel like I am never going to finish reading *Travels With Charley in Search of America* by John Steinbeck. It was written in the 1960s about a man who travels the country with his dog. They are on a completely different kind of journey than we are but it is still fun to read about it and see some of the similarities.

When we woke up the next day, it was a little warmer. We went for a 6-mile run. We had to find the trails on the other side of the lake. They were shorter, so we just did all of them. It was fun trying to find them. The trails were perfect running trails and it was so much fun exploring! The weather was ideal!

On the way back, we ran along the lake, and it was calling our name to SUP. So we went back to camp and inflated the iSUP. We only had to walk across the street to access deep enough water to put it in the creek that fed into the lake. We didn't have much time before we left so we only paddled a mile down the lake, but it was so worth it! We had the entire lake to ourselves! We paddled past the playground where a bus had dropped off a bunch of kids. They thought it was cool watching a dog was on a paddleboard.

I love watching people's faces when they see Jack perched on the front of the paddleboard. I'd like to think they are taking photos of me, but in reality, it is all about Jack. We stopped a few times and Jack and I went swimming in the lake since his belly was feeling better and the water was calm here. The water was surprisingly warm, and the lake was very clear. I didn't even have my bathing suit on, I went swimming in my clothes! It was awesome, we were in heaven!

Once again we were sad to leave this beautiful site. Checkout time was at 3 p.m. and we pulled out at 2:58 p.m. even though our camp hosts said that there was no hurry. I still had a little work to do so we stayed at the campground until 4 p.m. and then headed to the 81 North toward Annapolis. We wanted to leave late to beat the Washington D.C. traffic. Unfortunately, I forgot about Roanoke, Virginia. We went through there at 6 p.m., probably the worst time. We ended up being stuck in rush-hour traffic. There were a lot of trucks on the road. They wouldn't get out of the left hand lane so it was creating a traffic jam. It was a little annoying and I was wondering why they were doing that?

We got to the Washington D.C. area around 11 p.m. and wouldn't you know there was construction! There is no getting around traffic in that city! So what was to be a six-hour drive took eight hours. But that was ok. I was feeling happy and awake. We arrived at our next destination, Sport Fit Fitness Center, where we spent the night in the parking lot so we could see my old friend, Pete Cipolla, in the morning! We welcomed the next stops because we would be visiting friends and teaching another class.

Chapter 8: Maryland

I used to live in Maryland. I went to X-ray school here 24 years ago after moving from Pennsylvania where I grew up. I am familiar with the area but, of course, it has changed a lot since then. It was fun for me to be back and relive so many memories. My life was completely different back then. I used to work out with Pete and then he and I would go to the bar and drink all night. I used to drink a lot. I wasn't into outdoor sports like I am now. I worked out in the gym like many people on the East Coast, but my weekends would consist of getting crazy drunk in bars. I honestly don't know how I am still alive. I am ashamed to say that I wrecked my car seven times before I was 27 years old.

That's when I moved to San Diego. I never missed work, or got sick, so I thought that I was doing okay. Of course, at the time, I was also having a ton of fun. I quit drinking for good when I was 32 years old after getting a DUI and crashing my car into a parked car. I was a full time personal trainer at the time preaching a healthy life and here I was getting wasted with my clients on the weekends. I knew that I had a problem and I tried to stop drinking numerous times to no avail. I would try only drinking before I went out, then only drinking beer, then only drinking when I went out but nothing worked. After I had my first drink, there was no turning back. The night I got my DUI – on July 28, 2000 – I took my last drink. I realized if I ever hurt someone, I would never forgive myself. At that moment, I set my mind to quitting, and I have never had another alcoholic drink.

Pete's life has changed since those days as well. He is now married with two beautiful young girls. He arrived at the RV before his scheduled work time so we could visit for a while. It was fun to see him. Pete traveled part of the way to California with me when I moved there 20 years ago! It was a crazy time. We traveled in my little Honda Civic. I had everything I owned in there so space was tight. I only allowed Pete one small travel bag. He traveled with me from Maryland to Tennessee where he reluctantly flew home. We camped in a tent the entire way. Sometimes, we would pull over and just put the tent up in a field along the road!

As we visited this time, Pete showed me inside the gym where we had spent so much time together. The bar was no longer there, and they had expanded the gym. It was next to a huge park that I didn't even remember! We were both disappointed that we hadn't considered having me teach a dog fitness class here. It would have been really fun and something new for their members.

After our visit with Pete, we were off see our friend, Kelly Darrell in Annapolis! Kelly and her dog, Scooter, used to teach our Leash Your Fitness classes in San Diego until they moved to Annapolis last year. Kelly was a huge part of the growth of Leash Your Fitness. She started out as one of the class participants and loved it so much that she got her Group Fitness Certification and started teaching for me. She was a natural, and everyone loved her classes. She started a running class and helped inspire many people to start running. Everyone was very sad to see her move away, including me.

We hung out with her and her husband, Emrys, and Scooter all weekend at their house. They live walking distance from downtown Annapolis so we spent a lot of time walking. It was really pretty and there was plenty of water for Jack to swim! I was so excited to eat a Maryland crab cake again! When I lived in Maryland, I used to go crabbing and we would eat fresh crab and make delicious crab cakes. They definitely don't have the same kind in San Diego. Annapolis is a cute town full of little stores and ice cream. I love ice cream so I took advantage and had it twice while we were there!

It was perfect that Kelly and Emrys have SUPs as well so we all went SUPing! It was so fun seeing all of the large, beautiful houses on the water. Scooter loves to SUP, too, but he doesn't like to swim. That was fine until he fell in. Good thing he had his life jacket on so it was easy to get him back on the board. He was not happy and he looked terrified. It is funny how different two dogs can respond to water activity. Kelly was eight months pregnant. Seeing her on the board with wet and scared Scooter was too much to bear, so we headed back to the dock.

> **Even if your dog knows how to swim, you should have him wear a dog life jacket. These jackets feature a handle at the top that makes it easier to pull your dog out of the water and back onto your watercraft. Also, you never know about the currents or water conditions and the jacket helps to keep your dog buoyant and his head out of the water. If your dog doesn't like to swim, putting a life jacket on him will make him feel more secure in the water.**

The streets of Annapolis are very narrow so we were happy that there was a spot near their house where we could park Spirit for a few days. We had a good night sleep in a bed that night.

Saturday was hiking day! We went to a place called Quiet Waters. Since Kelly is pregnant, we didn't want to do anything too strenuous. It was a nice walk through the trees on some really nice trails, and Jack got to go swimming so he was happy!

Jack has been a tick magnet on this trip and we woke up to a huge one on his forehead. I was trying to find something natural for him since he is already on Revolution, a topical medication for fleas, ticks and heartworm. Obviously, he needed something else since it didn't seem to be working, and I was paranoid about Lyme disease on the East Coast. We stopped at Pet Barn, and I got him a special citronella shampoo and herbal powder called Tickz to put in his food. Believe it or not, I didn't find one more tick on him the entire trip!

Chapter 8: Maryland

The worst part of the day for Jack was getting the bath with the new shampoo. It was the first bath since the poop incident on our first day in New Mexico. Plus, I wanted Jack to look nice since we were going out for dinner with our friend, Doug Bopst, from Baltimore. We found a place near Kelly's where Doug met us. I am in a Fitness Business Mastermind Group, and Doug is in the same group with me. It was really interesting because Emrys is from Baltimore so they knew some of the same people! I am getting to see so many of my friends on this trip. It is fun to know people from all over the country.

> *I don't know why my mommy insists on making me smell like a flower. I am a dog and I like to be stinky. They should make dog shampoo that smells like horse poop. Then maybe I would like to get a bath!*

It was a good thing we met at a place with an awning because it started pouring down rain. We stayed there for a bit until it slowed down. The one thing about taking your dog to dinner with you is you have to sit outside. This usually isn't a problem in San Diego, but when you are other places in the country, it can get interesting! It was fun watching the rain and the people run through it!

The next day, we got up early to get ready for our fitness class at Dogwood Acres Pet Retreat. Wow! If you live in Annapolis or anywhere near it, you need to have your pup stay at this place! It is NICE! Plus, it has a bone-shaped swimming pool that Jack wanted to get into very badly. It also has an inside training room, which was a good thing because it was threatening rain and humid. There are several outside training yards, so we set up in two of them for the class. Kelly's mom, Barbara, drove up from St Mary's County to take the class and help out and she was a huge help. It was fun to see her as well!

The dogs were so good in class. They did drills, went over jumps and of course, worked on their basic commands. The rain held out for class, but it was a little humid so we still went inside for the stretching part at the end. By the time we got to the inside part of the class, all of the dogs were pooped! The inside felt good with the air conditioning. The dogs got to play a few more games, and they enjoyed their parents' company. They even entertained everyone with their shenanigans. The entertainment factor is the fun part about working out with your dog. The parents got to do doggy yoga and work on some balance drills. One of the men in class had a wife who had been following us on Instagram. She was away on travel so she made him go to class with their Westie. It was so cute, and we made sure to get a lot of photos to post for her to see!

The class was super fun and everyone left with a goody bag filled with One Dog Organic dog treats, a Kurgo collapsible bowl, a KIND bar, a pack of Sun Warrior Protein and lots of other fun stuff from Dogwood Acres. Four lucky people won the drawings. The participants all left happy with a few new exercises to try with their dogs. It was really fun working with the Erin from Dogwood Acres, and I really appreciated them having the class for us!

One of the girls that came to class was our friend, Priti Karnik. She is a veterinarian who used to live in San Diego. She and her dog, Kai, were regulars in our Leash Your Fitness classes. She had just recently moved to the Washington D.C. area after spending a few years in Saint Kitts teaching at a Veterinary School. It was too bad that she was on call because I was excited to see her new house and it was even on my way since I was heading to Pennsylvania after the class. Unfortunately, she had to hurry and get back to work after the class. Kelly and I were both thrilled that she came to class and, of course, Kai was excited to see Scooter and Jack.

Jack got to swim in the bone-shaped pool after class. He was such a good boy in class. He usually just sits on the sideline so I can demonstrate the exercises and make sure that everyone is implementing them correctly. When you have a class full of people exercising and dogs that you don't know, you have to be very aware of what is going on with no distractions.

It was so sad to leave Kelly. We had so much fun catching up on everything. Emrys is in the Navy so we are hoping that they move back to San Diego with their new baby after their time in Annapolis is done. We miss them very much!

Again, we were traveling on a Sunday, especially since we had to go through the beltway around Washington. So far we have scheduled it to be at friends' houses on the weekends, so it has been really easy to get campsites. It isn't the tourist season yet plus camping on a weekday has been great!

As mentioned, I am from Pennsylvania and my family was waiting patiently for our arrival. I hadn't been home since my mom passed away three years ago. It will be bittersweet to return but I am excited to see my family. They are really fun!

Chapter 9: Pennsylvania

W e arrived safely in West Newton, PA and have now traveled 3,326 miles. We have also spent over $1,100 on gas. That is okay because we are having so much fun. We are three weeks into our trip and it has been like heaven! I mentioned before the three great things about traveling in a RV. The two bad things are the toll road fees that cost more for RVs than cars and the low miles-per-gallon you get driving a RV. Thank goodness for the gas buddy app on my phone which helps me to find the cheapest gas, and for Costco app that helps me find if there are any Costco's on my route. They usually have the cheapest gas.

Seeing my family is always a treat. I have a very colorful family and there is never a dull moment when I am with them. I can count on plenty of hugs and laughter. Jack was not happy that the pool was not open yet. Last time we were here, he even went down the sliding board. He was the only dog ever to go in the pool. That shows how special he is!

The home where I grew up is on seven acres of land. We have a large pool, a pool house that has a full kitchen in it, a giant trampoline, a little basketball court and a golf cart that you can ride around the property. My brother, Randy, runs the family business, which is a service station, and he manages and lives on the property. When I was growing up, we had cattle and horses. Now he raises bison. His daughter, LeeAnne, loves animals so she is always rescuing some sort of critter. When we were there she had a pregnant kitty. Jack was happy that he got to follow the pregnant kitty around and sit and watch the bison. He wasn't sure what to do with them! He never bothers horses or other large animals. He mostly just ignores them.

We always refer to the family property as "the pool house" because that is where all of the action takes place. My family congregate there during the summer for picnics, pool parties or just to hang out. It is directly behind the service station. West Newton is a small town where everyone knows everyone, therefore there is always someone stopping by to say hi when they stop to get gas. That is where my class is going to take place in a few days.

My sister, Lynn, lives about 20 minutes away from where I grew up. It is a little larger area, but in Pennsylvania, nobody has fences. Everywhere is just like one large yard. So when we pulled into Lynn's house and they were not home yet, I started to clean out the RV. Jack and I would be staying there for almost a week, so it was a good time to clean house again. While I am emptying out the RV, Jack decided to go check out the neighbor's pool. He will not go in until I say it is okay, but he barks to let me know that he found something cool!

The neighbors came out and thought he was the cutest thing ever. They were more than happy to allow Jack in the pool, although they said it would be cold. It was toward the end of May so the water hadn't warmed up yet. Cold water doesn't bother Jack so I gave him the go ahead and he proceeded to entertain the neighbors with his "deck jumping." He jumps in from the side, swims to the stairs, gets out and then does it again and again and again! You get the picture!

One of the many perks in this cross country journey is that I got to spend time with my ever expanding family. Let me give you the quick introduction: I have 2 older brothers, Jack and Randy. Jack is married to Sue and they have 2 kids, Jason and Shalyn plus 3 grandchildren (my great nieces). Randy is married to Anne and they have 3 children named Randy, LeeAnne and Sara. I have one older sister, Lynn, who is married to Jack and they have 4 children named Ben, John, Andrew and Laura. Most of my nieces and nephews are grown and moved away, but a few of them were home during my visit. Shalyn lives there with her daughter, Alina. I went to Alina's school to watch her summer Olympics, but I was disappointed that I didn't get to see her dance while I was home because she is quite the entertainer. The timing just wasn't right for any of her recitals. Shalyn took me with them to get Alina's dance photos taken so at least I got to see her in her dance outfits. She is so beautiful, just like her mom! I also got to hang out with my other two nieces, Sara and LeeAnn a lot. We went and had ice cream two times! I think I mentioned that I love ice cream and it seems to run in my family! LeeAnn was in her first year of college and Sara in highschool but they still wanted to hang out with their Aunt Dawn and we had a great time with lots of laughs and talks about their future now that they were all grown up! They have turned out to be mature and beautiful girls and I am so proud of them. The bonus was we got to go see my cousin, Daneen, who has a clothing boutique called, Prima Diva Boutique. It is full of really cool and unique stuff.

In addition to my family, I got to hang out with my friends from high school. No matter how long we are apart, we start off right where we left off! One of them, Jackie, doesn't have kids, but she does have two Bernese Mountain Dogs that are her babies! My other two friends, Dawn and Terri, both have teenage kids so their lives are completely different from mine, but we still love to get together. We chatted about old times and went through our old photo albums and laughed about all of the crazy things that we used to do! I love hearing what their kids are up to and what they have going on in their lives. Terri was actually going to be a Grandma soon! Going home is always a treat for me and everyone goes out of their way to spend time with me while I am there and I really appreciate it. I feel very fortunate to have such a loving family and friends!

One day, we went on a field trip. My two nieces, my sister, her friend, my friend and I (and Jack) all piled in the RV and went on a field trip to Critter Country! Critter Country saves animals from zoos that are going out of business and other places where the animals are not treated well. They rely solely on donations and people like us paying to visit. The animals are treated well and loved. Most of them just roam freely in the fenced in fields. We got to feed a lot of them, there was a pig named Scooter and furry chickens. The lemurs were fun, especially the little baby riding on her mommy's back!

We got to see zebras, camels, bears, wolves, tigers, pigs, lemurs and all kinds of different monkeys. My friend, Laurie, is the owner with her husband, Rob and Laurie was even playing with a 4-month-old Leopard! It was a lot of fun. Jack waited in Spirit for us. It would have been interesting to see how he would react around some of the animals, but of course there was a no dog policy and for good reason. He has already seen many of those animals while we have been hiking. When we were in Idaho, we came upon a Moose and her babies and we saw a Bear on a nearby trail near Mt. Shasta. He was nose to nose with a deer in the Mammoth area of California. The deer there were so used to people that I was feeding them carrots out of my hand! We have seen coyotes, bobcats and even a mountain lion on our neighborhood trails in San Diego. And, of course, he has seen cows, horses and bison. The meanest animal we have yet to see is a wild turkey. You will hear about that soon!

When mommy went to Critter Country, I saw her holding a chicken. I had mixed feelings about having a brother that was a chicken so I am really happy that she didn't bring him on the rest of our journey with us!

After our visit to Critter Country, it was time for our class with all of my friends and family. They have been curious as to what Leash Your Fitness is all about, so I thought it would be fun to have a class while I was home. I have to admit that I was a little concerned because none of the dogs had any training and some had never even been on a leash! Remember I am from the country where dogs roam free. It is a good thing that I have a lot of experience so I knew what to do because it was crazy at the start. We had dogs trying to fight with each other, dogs pulling their moms arms off and dogs not wanting to do anything.

The class went really well, though, and everyone had a great time. We played games, did drills, exercises and a little yoga. At the end of class, I wasn't sure who was more tired, the dogs or the people! We also had a huge audience watching. All of my family, including my aunts and uncles, came to watch.

It was the first time since my mom passed away that we were all together. My mom must have been happy because in the middle of the class we looked up and there was an upside down rainbow over us. There was no rain in the forecast and the sky was blue. It was the first time in my life I have ever seen an upside down rainbow. Of course, everyone started crying tears of joy that my parents were with us again. It was a very memorable moment on my trip and just proof that my travel spirits really were with me.

I think that everyone left that class with a new appreciation for their dogs. They didn't think that their dogs knew how to do basic obedience, but we showed them that they really do! We like to educate people that your dog WANTS to learn new things.

Dogs want to think and have a job to do. If your dog is barking, chewing, and acting out, it is usually because he/she is bored and needs some mental stimulation. Just teaching them basic dog obedience and maybe even a few tricks will really help!

While we were in Pennsylvania, we decided to get the oil changed in the RV, the tire pressure checked and all of the fluids topped off. I took Jack to the veterinary clinic to make sure he was okay. He was having belly issues back in Virginia. They seemed to be better but I just wanted to make sure. The veterinarian said that sometimes dogs can get colitis from swimming in strange places. Fortunately, everything checked out well on both the RV and on Jack!

We had such a good time in Pennsylvania. Everyone loved seeing Spirit all decorated for our Jack's Journey USA tour and of course they loved meeting Jack. We did a lot of different things with my family while we were there. Jack is such a good boy; he just goes along with everything that I do and everyone loves to meet him. Just another reason it pays to have a well-behaved dog welcomed in many places.

Three years earlier, my mom passed away in the hospital. She had a routine hiatal hernia repair and the surgeon made a mistake and it cost my mom's life. Her death was a shock to us all. My mom was a very active 82-year-old. Everyone loved her. She was like an angel, always helping people. I was at work waiting to hear from my sister that my mom came out of the surgery all right. Instead, I got the call that she died in the recovery room. It was a very dark time for me. I was angry for a long time. I took it out on those I loved and I had a really hard time dealing with it. I flew home that night for the funeral and stayed a week to help my sister clean out my mom's apartment. It was a very sad time for my family. When I left Pennsylvania, I honestly didn't know if I could ever go back. My mom was the glue in our family. She was active in everyone's lives and she was well loved by everyone.

I am really happy that I went back home. Family is so important and whether you love your family or just tolerate them, they are a part of who you are. I think that they are a very important part of our life. I am sad that they live so far away, and value my time with them and I am glad we got to spend a week hanging out and having fun but its time to move on. They have their lives to live and we have more places to visit.

We are off to see my sister's summerhouse in Chautauqua, New York. I have never been there. Her house is on a lake, and now is our chance to have fun together!

Chapter 10: New York

I was very sad leaving my family because I don't have any idea when I will see them again. As my niece would say, I was a "hot mess" when I left. I couldn't stop crying. Between the upside down rainbow and saying goodbye to everyone, it was very emotional for me. Our lives are very different and everyone is busy. My nieces and nephews are all moving away and going to college or starting their careers. I see my sister, Lynn, the most. We get together once a year and go somewhere fun. Of course, this year I came to her so that was a relief that I was still going to see her one more time!

The drive to Chautauqua was super easy, and Jack LOVED Lynn's lake house. There were plenty of squirrels to chase and, of course, there was a dock and water! We went down to the lake as soon as we arrived, and Jack showed off his dock diving ability for all of the neighbors. He didn't care that the water was cold. He loves to swim in all water. Once, in Lake Shasta, it was snowing and he was in the river swimming!

One thing for sure, Jack sleeps really well every night. We stay pretty active all day long so he goes to bed a tired boy. Even on our drive days, we do something when we arrive at our destination.

The next day, we woke to a chilly 31 degrees! So instead of heading for the lake, we went for a long walk around the neighborhood and met the nice neighbors. Then we walked around The Chautauqua Institute.

According to its website, The Institution, originally the Chautauqua Lake Sunday School Assembly, was founded in 1874 as an educational experiment in out-of-school, vacation learning. It is a now a not-for-profit, 750-acre educational center beside Chautauqua Lake in southwestern New York State, where approximately 7,500 persons are in residence on any day during a nine-week season, and a total of over 100,000 attend scheduled public events.

You usually have to have a pass to enter the Institute, but the season wasn't open yet so no pass was needed, and we practically had the place to ourselves! Lynn's husband, Jack, grew up every summer in the Institute. His family still has a house there, which is how Lynn and Jack ended up buying a house nearby. There are some very old houses in the Institute.

Since it was too windy and cold to SUP, we decided to go check out a hike at the Chautauqua Gorge. We had a hard time finding it but once we did, it was a nice hike down to a river where Jack got to swim. One thing is for sure, we find water everywhere! That is how he has been able to swim in every state that we have ever visited!

Chapter 10: New York

There were a bunch of people camping and singing songs and everyone was so happy! It was Memorial Day weekend so there was an extra amount of people out enjoying the great outdoors! We love that! Lynn had never been to this trail so now she has a new place to bring visitors too. Once again, we inspired someone to try something new as my sister spends most of her time golfing!

One of the things we do as a family is play games. I miss that in San Diego. My friends and I never get together to play games, and I love playing games. During our visit, we played Yahtzee and Skat with Jack's sister and her husband who were visiting from Florida. It was a bonus seeing them!

The stay would not have been complete without teaching Lynn to SUP. When we woke up on Sunday and it was sunny and warm, we inflated the SUP and walked to the nearest dock. Lynn was a natural, and she loved it. Jack even took a ride with her! While Jack and I paddled across the lake, Lynn went in the house and ordered a iSUP just like ours from our friends at ISLE with our discount code (Leash75)! It is perfect for the lake there because it is easy to carry, super stable for the rough water when it is windy, and she can deflate it and take it to Florida with her when they go to their winter house.

We had a really full and fun couple of days in Chautauqua. Once again, we were sad to leave! There seems to be a trend that everywhere that we go, we hate to leave. We must move on to our friend Kelli's house because she is going to host one of our Leash Your Fitness classes! We can't wait to say that we taught a class in Rome!

Since we got a late start from Lynn's house, we didn't arrive in New Hartford, New York until 5:30 p.m., just in time for dinner at Kelli's friend's house! What a nice group of ladies. They had a big yard for Jack to run around in after our drive and they welcomed us with open arms. The ladies loved hearing about our adventures so far and we loved hearing their funny stories! I haven't laughed that hard in a long time! It was a great way to start our visit here!

Kelli insisted on us staying in her house instead of the RV. Kelli has an Australian Shepard puppy named Cody. Jack had to let Cody know who was boss. He went in the house and straight to the dog toy box like he always does in every house that we go to. He took out all of the chew toys and laid next to him so Cody couldn't get to them. The funny part is that Jack never plays with chew toys. Then he guarded the toy box so that Cody couldn't get to any of his toys. To top it off, he guarded Cody's food so that he couldn't eat. What a spoiled brat! The funny part was that Cody didn't even care. He just kept trying to play with Jack, but Jack didn't want any part of that!

It is so fun to visit people who have dogs. The first thing that I do is go find the toy box. It is so fun to play with other dog's toys. They have so many cool smells on them. I don't destroy them like some of my friends do. I just play with them and keep them all to myself.

The next day was really exciting! We got to go hiking in the Adirondacks! Kelli, her three kids and Cody, and her friend went so once again, we all piled into Spirit. What a cool experience that was. It was a beautiful drive up into the mountains and the trails were so perfect! The view from the top was amazing! We sat up there for a long time and chatted.

We had a big group hiking with us because Kelli's other friends met us there. I was very nervous about the tick problem so I felt bad but I kept Jack on the leash most of the time so that he would stay on the trail. The other dogs were used to it so they were running around but Jack didn't seem to mind. Kelli was telling me how bad the ticks have been. They used to never be up there but now they are and a lot of the dogs have Lyme disease. Jack didn't get any so my preventative measures must be working. She had also warned me about the bugs, but they didn't seem to bother me. We aren't used to bugs in San Diego. We do have ticks but they don't normally carry Lyme disease. It is mainly an East Coast disease, for now anyway!

A good habit to have is to check your dog after every hike to make sure that everything is ok. Check his paws to make sure that there are no rocks or anything stuck between his pads. Check his skin for ticks or any burrs.

We were so happy that Kelli's friend came on the hike with us. Not only was she fun to hike with, she had a dock on one of the beautiful lakes, so guess where we went after the hike? Jack was once again excited and showed off for everyone. They thought it was so funny. Jack even inspired Cody to go in the water! Maybe he will become the next dock diving dog! He usually doesn't go in but step-by-step, he went in the water. Jack had fun playing with his Kong Wubba, but at one point, he was shaking so bad from the water being so cold that I made him get out. I threw the Wubba in the yard – a bit too high – and it landed on the roof of the house. Kelli, being the awesome lady that she is, got it down for us with a kayak paddle! Jack was once again happy!

We had another full and fun day. Jack is having the time of his life on this journey. I often wonder what I would do differently if he wasn't here and then I remember that I probably wouldn't be on this trip to begin with if it wasn't for him. He has definitely had a profound impact on my life, and I enjoy every day with him.

We got to go to work with Kelli the next morning. She has a fitness studio so it was the first time in a long time that I did a workout indoors. All of Kelli's clients were so nice to Jack and I at the studio. It is no surprise that she has amazing people around her because she is one of the most inspiring and positive people that I know. She has a beautiful smile and she makes everyone around her feel special. Her clients love her and so do we!

We were excited to meet her other clients, the ones with dogs at our Leash Your Fitness Class. Kelli was hosting a class for the Freedom Dog Project, an organization that trains service dogs for the military. It was perfect since it was the day after Memorial Day! The class was in Rome, New York, so now we can say we taught in Rome! We even made the front page of the Rome newspaper! We had a great turnout and even people without dogs came to watch. Everyone was amazed at how the dogs listened so well in class and quickly learned what to do. Many went from being hyper and unable to sit, to sitting on command and calming down with each exercise. I gave a lot of dog tips so that everyone had something to do for homework with their dogs.

All ages came to the class! We had little girls and puppies. We had older people and big dogs. We like to prove that you are never too young or old or too big or small to have fun getting fit and learning new things! The best part was that we raised over $400 for the Freedom Dog Project! We hope that helps them in some small way and will pay it forward to help others in need of a service dog so they, too, can lead a normal life.

We were all very tired after our busy day. It was hot and humid there and that tires you out too. Californians are not used to that! We are spoiled with perfect weather and that is another reason for the journey. We want to see how incorporating outdoor fitness into different areas will work with the different climates. So far, we haven't had a problem, but it isn't summer yet.

The next morning, I got up early and got a lot of Internet work done before I packed up and headed to our next stop. I never know if I am going to have WiFi or any cell coverage at the campground and I don't like to get behind on things. The next stop was a total mystery. We just started driving East and kind of made it up as we went! We just knew that our next stop was on the way to Boston where Kurgo and The Fish and Bone, a dog boutique in Boston were hosting a Leash Your Fitness class at the Hill House Backyard Dash. We ended up in a really interesting campground – well, kind of!

Chapter 11: New Hampshire

Not sure why we had the most frustrating travel day yet. Nothing seemed to work out. The GPS kept taking us the freeway route even though I had set it for a route without a freeway. We like to see things, even if it isn't always the fastest route and our GPS doesn't agree! Now that we are on the East Coast, it is confusing because the states are smaller and I forgot about Vermont. I would put in a city in New Hampshire and the GPS wouldn't recognize it but that is because really the city was in Vermont! I finally figured out that little mishap. Then we would stop for gas and because of the stringent restrictions on gas stations, the gas pump would turn off every few seconds. Do you know how much gas Spirit takes? It was taking forever to get gas and beyond frustrating.

One of the problems was that I didn't even know where we were going. I had a few lakes in mind but I was trying to figure out which one was on the way to where we were going, and since the GPS would not recognize the addresses, we had to just figure it out as we went. We stopped at a lake in Vermont and were just going to stay there, but the campground wasn't on the lake. Jack got to swim anyhow because the rule is, he gets to swim in EVERY state that we pass through. It was a bonus to pass a lake because we needed a break from the drive anyhow, and the lake was pretty.

We finally decided on Greenfield Lake that was suggested by Josee Dupont, a friend of Kelli's who likes to SUP with her dogs. She lives nearby and loves the lake. We finally arrived after six hours of travel. We couldn't wait to check out the lake!

We arrived at the campground and there were no campers in the entire park! We parked Spirit in a campsite that looked like it had a trail down to the lake. We walked through a trail to the "lake" but it was really only a gross duck pond and the trail was pretty overgrown. Jack and I were both disappointed with this find after our confusing travel day, so we decided to just drive down to the parking lot by the beach and check it out. The icing on the cake of today was the sign that said, "NO DOGS." Since there was nobody in the entire campground, we walked right past the sign and went to the little beach so Jack could go swimming! There are certain things you just HAVE to do!

The lake was super pretty and calling our name so we inflated the SUP and were ready to go check out the lake when it started thundering! By this time, I just started laughing! What the heck was the universe trying to tell us today? It was just a really frustrating day at every turn! We went in the water for a few minutes anyhow until the thunder starting sounding closer and then headed back to the parking lot just in time for the downpour!

Since it was pouring down rain and there was nobody around the entire park, I decided to just camp out in the parking lot! It was flat, near the beach and lake and the campground didn't have hookups anyhow. So, why not?

Our campsite worked out great! The next morning was BEAUTIFUL! We started our day with an early morning SUP around the entire lake (2.3 miles), stopping to swim a few times. The water was really warm! It was also really clear. We could see the bottom in some spots. What a relaxing way to start the day!

The day was a good beach day so we got the beach chair out and a few snacks. Then we strolled past the NO DOGS sign and spent the entire day on the beach. I attempted to read my book but Jack had other ideas in mind. He was non-stop crazy with his Wubba. I didn't get much reading done because I was constantly throwing the toy for him. I would mix it up and sometimes throw it on the beach and sometimes in the water. I would throw it in different directions - anything to make him think AND to make it take him longer to bring it back. He would bring it back and lay it by my feet. If I ignored him, he would nudge it closer, sometimes he would dig a hole around it and throw sand on me. I had to laugh! He is so entertaining to watch!

A few people walked by and they confirmed that is was okay for me to be on the beach. Everything was basically closed for the season so nothing was being enforced. It was also a weekday so there were not a lot of people or staff around. They had a little day use area that was on the other side of the beach where people were walking. I talked to a few guys who were there enjoying the park. They couldn't believe how obsessed Jack was with his Wubba. They even threw it a few times for him. Jack confirmed that although he is 10 years old, he still has a lot of energy to burn!

Another short storm rolled through, so we went back to the RV in the parking lot and hung out in there for a bit. I got some computer stuff caught up and organized. I have been visiting people for the last two weeks, so I needed a down day to get things caught up and to be alone with Jack. He likes having mommy time! As much as I love my friends and family, it was nice to be back in Spirit and on the road finding new adventures.

After the storm was done, we took a run through the campground to check it out. Greenfield Lake State Park is a really large park. The campsites are wooded and spaced out. There were just three campers in the entire park and we never saw them at the beach. They must have just been at their sites the entire time. The most exciting thing that happened is that we got chased by a wild turkey! We have seen bears, moose, coyotes, bob cats, mountain lions, deer and elk on trails and have never had a problem and now we almost get attacked by a crazy TURKEY! It wasn't leaving us alone! I was trying to take photos of it, but I was frightened! I started throwing sticks toward it so it would stop chasing us and finally we outran it. I wish I would have taken some video of the crazy thing! There is never a dull moment with us!

We survived that and headed back to camp. It was super humid and now I was all sweaty so we went back to the lake to go for a swim to get rinsed off with my biodegradable soap. I didn't know at the time that I could have just gone to take a shower in the bathrooms that were open. I ran right by them and just assumed that they weren't open since I didn't see any staff and there weren't many campers. Never assume anything!

I get back to the RV. It was a mess because I threw everything in there when it started raining! I was trying to get it organized because I am a neat freak and I don't like it when things are out of place. Of course, at the worst possible time, we had our first visitor on our trip! Josee, who told us about the camp, came by to visit as she lives nearby. I was so embarrassed by the state of the RV but she didn't care! She was one of the coolest people and super nice, which doesn't surprise me since she is a friend of Kelli's. It was so fun to meet her. She is a remarkable lady who does a lot of dog rescue. She also loves to SUP with her dogs. What a perfect person to meet! We love meeting new people, especially when they love dogs!

What a great day, the frustrating travel day was worth it! It was like we had our own private beach and camp! We ended up camping in the parking lot another night! Why not?

The next morning, we decided to take off early to head to our next stop. I went to the beach and did my yoga stretches and threw the toy for Jack a few more times. It is hard to leave our own private beach, but it was once again time to move on! We noticed people walking from the showers as we left so I decided to take a hot shower and wash my hair. It felt so good! I could have taken a shower in the RV but I just didn't want to use all of the water in the tank. We stopped at the office on the way out. It wasn't open, so we put money for our "campsite" in the envelope in the after-hours slot. While at the dump station, we finally saw a park worker. He asked us if we were camping there since I was using the dump station. I told him I just did for two nights! I just didn't tell him which site - the "parking lot" site.

We were off to our friend, Lisa's house in Planstow, New Hampshire. Lisa moved back to New Hampshire five weeks ago from San Diego! How perfect is that? The really perfect part is that she is a dog groomer and Jack needed another haircut so it was perfect timing! Another plus was that I didn't think I would get to see her since she is north of Boston, our next stop. But since I didn't really want to drive into Boston, and I had arranged a ride into the city for the class tomorrow, it all worked out perfectly!

The drive to Lisa's work was super simple, much better than our last drive. That was a total fluke day and those kinds of days make you appreciate the good ones. Looking back, that day actually wasn't all that bad. Things can always be worse!

We showed up to her work, Free Dog, and we had an audience! Everyone came out to welcome Jack and I. It was so nice! It was fun to see Lisa and she had her dogs, G and Mira, at work with her so it was like a little reunion! I was going to drop Jack off and go into the town to post some blogs and get some work done, but they had a really nice deck there and gave me their Internet access, so I set up shop on the deck. I ended up just staying there all day working while Lisa finished her shift. It was a very pretty setting, plus the girls were so nice. They took their break and came out to chat with me. Jack looked so handsome after his haircut, and although he won't ever admit it, I know he felt better, too! Plus, we will be able to find any ticks much easier now!

I won't even admit this to my mom but I love it when I get my haircut. I don't like the process of getting a bath and for someone touching me but I always feel so good afterwards. It makes me feel like a puppy again!

When Lisa got done with work, we headed back to her house so she could get a shower. It was close by and they had a nice flat driveway for me to park Spirit. Then we headed into Newburyport for dinner. We ate at a super cute dog-friendly restaurant that was very healthy and good! After dinner we took a walk along the water. We officially made it to the East Coast! We can see the Atlantic Ocean!

Chapter 12: Boston

Jack and I slept in the RV last night because we knew we had to get up early to take off to Kurgo headquarters to meet Jennifer. I was having an anxiety attack about driving Spirit into Boston so Jennifer, from Kurgo, offered to pick us up! Kurgo came on board as one of my sponsors after I had contacted them to tell them about my journey. They provide gear that make outdoor adventures with your dog safer and more enjoyable. They are also all about traveling safely with your dog and so they were all for helping me out since our journey was all about outdoor activities! The headquarters is north of Boston so I parked Spirit there for the day. It worked out great because once we arrived in Boston we found out that there were very low underpasses. We would not have fit under them. Plus the roads are very narrow roads and there was no parking. I do not like driving into cities in my car let alone my RV!

Our event was with Kurgo and The Fish and Bone, a small dog boutique in Boston. It was being held at the Hill House Back Yard Dash on the Esplanade. The Hill House Back Yard Dash was a family and dog-friendly 5-K with fun activities in the park afterwards. It was pretty funny because we had to drive the car on to the Esplanade over a small bridge and onto the grass. Jennifer and I felt like Thelma and Louise! It was just another adventure to remind me of how much fun this journey is and how each day is a surprise! There is no way that Spirit was going to do that so I was so thankful that Jennifer picked me up!

We couldn't have asked for a better day! The sun was shining, but it was very warm, a little too warm for the dogs. We helped to set up the booth and then Jack and I went off to explore Boston!

We took a stroll up Newbury Street and saw all of the trendy shops. Then we went to the famous Boston Commons. I got lemonade from a street vendor, and we walked around the park. We even stopped by the famous bar from the television show, Cheers. Jack liked the part when he was able to dock dive in the Charles River to cool off. He had an audience watching him jump off the dock, swim to shore, run back up to the dock and then jump again! It makes people smile when they see him do things like that, and I like to show him off.

The class wasn't scheduled until 1 p.m. and by then it was very hot. We are all about safety for the dogs so we found a shaded area and had a lot of fun teaching the class participants some exercises that they could do on their dog walks including yoga stretches. The class went well and everyone loved it. One woman even did the class in her dress and flip-flops! They asked when we would be back for another class. Next time we do a road trip, we are going to stay in each place longer since everyone keeps asking us to stay. They find out how fun the class is and then they think of other people that would have enjoyed it.

It is very important to remember that your dog does not wear shoes like you do. On hot summer days, remember that the pavement is hot. Always touch the back of your hand on the pavement to test it before you take your dog for a walk. If it is too hot to your touch, keep your dog on the grass and not on the sidewalk. Even sand and dirt trails can get too hot for your dog to walk on.

We had a little lab puppy in class that stole the show! Starbuck had everyone stopping to pet his little furry head. He was so darn cute! Everyone left happy with a goody bag and some new exercises and ideas to work on.

After class, Jennifer took us back to Kurgo. It was really fun spending the morning with her. She was a big help in planning classes for us and very generous in supplying class prizes for all of our classes. We want to thank Kurgo for believing in our mission, helping us to stay safe and being a part of our journey!

Chapter 13: Maine

After Jennifer dropped us off, Jack and I headed to Biddeford, Maine! I couldn't believe we were in Maine! I had always wanted to go to Maine and we were there. We drove straight to the site of tomorrow's class and pre-ran the trail so that we knew what to expect. Kurgo and Super Dogs and Cats are sponsoring the class on the Eastern Trail. The trail is a flat and wide trail, perfect for our Walking Woof Workout.

It had been a long and hot day and all I wanted to do was take a shower. We drove to Old Orchard Beach and found a campground. We arrived around 7 p.m. to find out that they only allow couples and families to stay the night. WHAT? Is that even legal? We have never even heard of that! He said most of the campgrounds in that area had similar rules, and I was so tired I didn't feel like shopping around. I talked the guy into letting us stay only after he called the owner and couldn't get in touch with him. Didn't he know that Jack and I are family? The campground was practically empty. It was the strangest thing but nothing surprised me at that point! I was just thankful for a hot shower because I was pretty gross!

The next morning, it was threatening rain. I laid in bed and prayed for my weather spirits to hold the rain off until 10 a.m. when the class was over. We arrived at the trailhead to a lot of excited people and dogs. We knew it was going to be a fun group! Our friend, Lisa, had driven up from New Hampshire with her friends and it was nice to have a familiar face in class.

It was a very large class, but the trail was wide with not many people on it so it was perfect! The dogs were kept on leash during class and we went over different exercises and obedience drills to add to their dog walks. It started getting really cloudy so we headed back toward the beginning of the trail to end the class with yoga stretches.

My weather spirits came true! Just as the class was ending, it started to sprinkle. We hurried up and got the group photos taken and did the raffle drawing back in the parking lot, and it started to POUR DOWN RAIN!! It was crazy! It was perfect timing!

It was a super fun class and the first 10 to show up got goodie bags filled with gifts from our sponsors. A few people wanted to purchase Jack's Journey USA t-shirts so it was funny having them and their dogs in the RV during a rainstorm. We aren't used to that in San Diego so it was really an adventure! After class, we hung out in the parking lot for about an hour and organized everything. It was a real mess after all of that, plus I didn't want to drive in the pouring rain AND I had to go back out on the trail to pick up the pile of poop bags that we left at the trailhead. Remember to always keep the trails clean!

Chapter 13: Maine

We were now off to Acadia National Park. Acadia is one of the only national parks that is dog friendly and I was so excited to check it out. Everyone that I knew suggested that I go there because it was so beautiful. I was intrigued to see what it was all about. It was crazy how the temperature plummeted on the drive from Biddeford to Acadia. It was time to pull out the rain and winter gear and put the shorts away for a bit!

We weren't sure where to camp so I found a campsite on the Go Pet Friendly site called Hadley's Point Campground. It was a few miles west of Acadia, so we stopped there. It was on the expensive side but it was family owned and everyone was super nice. Plus, it had full hookups, WiFi and a laundry. SCORE! It was a huge campground. Since it was pouring down rain and I had laundry to do, we found an end spot in the grass near the laundry. It was not their tourist season yet, so there were plenty of sites available.

The campground was perfect for us. It had WiFi so I could get work done, a laundry so we could get clean towels (they were getting pretty nasty from Jack swimming and getting them all dirty), and it was a nice campground to take a walk in when it stopped raining. We noticed that there was a guy and his dog staying in a tent near us. We felt bad for them because he had his stuff all over the picnic table, and it was getting all wet. He wasn't "home" when we walked past or we would have had him come hang out with us for a while. We like meeting new people!

I woke up the next morning and it was POURING down rain! Man, I don't ever think I heard it rain so hard. It probably sounds worse when you are laying in a RV. It was cold, too.

The heater in Spirit kept coming on. We decided THIS was the day to sleep in! It was nice to just lie in bed and relax and read my book with no agenda. The last few days had been pretty busy. I was now reading a book about Alaska and dog sledding. It was really good so I wasn't too upset about the rain.

Monday, June 1 - *It is officially five weeks into our trip, the half way point and the furthest spot from San Diego! We have traveled 4,600 miles, and I am feeling so blessed. It has been such an adventure. So far, everything is going perfect. No RV mechanicals, no health issues and we are meeting amazing people along the way! I feel so fortunate to get to spend quality time with Jack and we are both having such a great time!*

It never stopped raining so at noon, we decided to take a drive to Bar Harbor. Bobby, in the office gave me some good pointers on where to go. I loved talking to the ladies in the office, they were so nice! I had to get a lobster roll because that is what you do in Maine. I hadn't eaten out much so far, but the lobster roll was a must, and, of course, we had to make that part of our adventure. Jack and I walked around the town in the rain and asked everyone in every shop that we went into who had the best lobster rolls. Everyone gave us a different answer. I finally decided on a little deli because the guy inside was nice to Jack, let him come in out of the rain and even gave him a biscuit. The roll was good and loaded with lobster. I don't like mayonnaise so I had it warm with no mayonnaise. I am always "that person" who never gets anything the way it is listed on the menu. I always have to alter something! On the other hand, Jack was happy with his biscuit just the way it was!

Bar Harbor is like any other tourist town with the tourist shops and restaurants, except the view is incredible, even in the rain. It is only a few minutes from Acadia National Park and even though it was raining, we were excited to go check it out!

Acadia was a little confusing to drive in. There were one way roads and because of the height restrictions on a few of the bridges, we were a little limited as to where we could go. We started to drive up Cadillac Mountain, but quickly realized it was so foggy that it was going to be a waste of time. So we turned around and headed back down the mountain.

Our first stop was Sieur De Monts, which was recommended by our friend, Cathy Hardalo. We hiked up Dorr Mountain in the rain. There is no reason you can't get out and do fun things when it is raining. The saying goes, "There is no bad weather, only bad clothes," and I was excited to get to wear my new rain boots!

The hike up Dorr Mountain was loaded with rock steps! I bet there were 300 of them. Cathy, a client from our class in San Diego, told us about this hike. I think she was getting me back for making her do so many training hills and stairs in San Diego! It was a really fun hike and the best part was on the way back down, it cleared up and we got a super view of the harbor. That was a bonus!

After the hike, we drove to the end of the park to Seal Beach, which was not dog friendly, so we didn't hang out there. We then headed over to Northeast Harbor and checked out all of the lobster boats. I had never been in a national park quite like this one. There are many entrances to the park from the road and there are no gates to go through, so technically you can drive through it for free. You do have to have a park pass in your window if you park anywhere. We weren't there in the tourist season so the parking lots and roads were pretty empty. The rules may be stricter during the tourist season.

The next day it was pouring again so I figured we might as well take advantage of the laundry and leave here with clean clothes! It seemed to be the place to hang out on a cold, wet morning! We met the owner, and he told us stories about his rescued Pit bull and how the campground had been passed down through the generations. They were the third generation to own it, which I thought was pretty cool. Some of the ladies in the office were from the first generation! You could tell it was a well taken care of campground and that everyone that worked there loved it.

We also met the guy and his dog that were staying in the tent. I didn't think he was home again because the grey car that had been parked there wasn't there, but I came to find out that wasn't his car. The guy, whose name was Ted, was actually blind! It was so fun to talk to him and find out his story.

Ted and Lapsi, his Labrador Retriever, are a team. Ted went completely blind at the beginning of the year after years of his eyes progressively getting worse. He had very little "light" sight. He was going through a tough time including a divorce, no job and no place to live. We decided to hang out with him and Lapsi for a few hours in the laundry. It was warm and dry in there. I read a few poems that he had written which he hadn't read in a long time and we just listened to his stories. He also told us some hikes to go on since he grew up in the area. It makes you think how your life would change if you suddenly went blind.

Ted was a super nice guy. He had two little girls and wanted to show them that you should never give up, no matter what! The rain let up so we walked him back to his camp. He gave me a little driftwood, sea glass ornament that he made. It was really cool and I keep it in Spirit to remind me of the amazing people that we met on our journey. We gave him some KIND bars and some One Dog Organic treats for Lapsi. We also gave him a little cash to help him out which he did not want to take. I told him it was for Lapsi so he couldn't refuse it! It was sad to leave him, and I wish there was a way to keep in touch with him because he was such a cool guy. He was going to go look at an apartment, so hopefully that will be a new start for him. We hope so!

Meeting cool people like Ted is what makes traveling such an adventure. It is another reason that I like to travel alone because I feel like I talk to more people. Everyone has a story that got them to where they are. Sometimes the story is sad. Sometimes it is inspiring. Sometimes it is educational, but most of the time it is just good to hear. We often get so caught up with our own lives that it is good to hear what other people have going on. If there is one trait that I got from my parents that I love is the ability to talk to anyone. I seriously couldn't imagine coming on a trip like this without talking to people. It is so interesting and fun to meet so many people from all over! My dad used to say that my mom was the only person he knew that could talk to a wrong number for an hour! I definitely got that trait from her, my boyfriend says it always takes longer to go hiking with me because I talk to everyone on the trail!

Ted told us to go to Bubble Rock so that is where we headed. He said they used to party up there when they were kids. It is so crazy to think that people actually grow up in a national park!

Bubble Rock was a huge boulder that was teetering off of the side of another huge boulder. Unlike the hike yesterday, this one was pretty tame. I met a family up at the top from Texas. The kids were trying to push the huge boulder over the cliff. I am sure that happens every day and they were having a great time. I love to see families out hiking and enjoying the outdoors.

We went down the Bubble Rock trail that was a different way than we went up. It was a crazy rock garden with a great view of the lake. It was pretty foggy, but the view was worth it. The hikes in the park were anything but normal. I have hiked all over the country and I had never seen anything like the hikes here. You never know what you are going to get. Jordan Lake was at the bottom of the trail and, unfortunately, it was one of the lakes where dogs were not allowed to swim. We took the Jordan Pond Trail back to the car. It took us up a creek bed where Jack, at least, got his feet wet in the freezing water.

After the hike, we had to take a break and warm up in the RV. We had a bite to eat and dried off and then continued on to our next adventure. Jack is thinking, "Yippee! What is next?" This is another reason I like to travel alone. I like to make the most out of every day, and there are very few people who can keep up. Jack is always ready to go, so he makes a great travel partner!

I may be 10 years old but I love to stay active. I came on this journey fit but I think I am now in the best shape of my life. I am having so much fun swimming, hiking and hanging out with my mom. There is always something fun to do everywhere that we go!

We stopped at Jordan Pond House. They are known for their afternoon teatime with homemade popovers. We didn't get there until after 5 p.m., so they were closed, but it was a cute place. We headed up Penobscot Trail. Wow!! We thought that the other trails were a challenge! This one was really crazy! I had to lift Jack up because the rocks were pretty high. There were railings and handholds and it was really steep. I would not recommend this trail for a beginner hiker or anyone with a large dog. The start of the hike would definitely weed out the beginners. After the high rocks, railings and handholds, the trail turned pretty normal. Near the top it was all steep slate. Remember that it was cold and rainy and I was in my rain boots! Thank goodness the trail was well marked with blue paint markers and cairns or else we would have had no idea where to go. There wasn't anyone else on this trail. The moss on the slate was really pretty. It looked like someone splattered paint on it. The slate seemed to go on forever. I felt like I was on another planet. I forgot to take Jack's booties and it was cold and wet on his paws. Even though he wasn't complaining, I picked him up a few times to give his paws a break.

We finally arrived at the top. It was windy and freezing!! I took a few selfies next to the sign to prove that we made it. I was bummed that it was so foggy because we couldn't see the view. It was so cold that my phone froze and turned off after we took the photo at the top. Since I was using the GPS on the phone with my Map My Run app, and I am not the best at reading maps, we took the wrong turn on the way back down. The slate went as far as you can see so it was not hard to do. I got a little nervous when I realized we were going the wrong way, and it was getting dark.

I had a trail map but because it was so windy and raining, it was in shreds. Luckily, I could patch it back together, and I figured out where we were and where we had to go. It ended up working out better as things often do. We didn't have to go back down that crazy rocky beginning section. We ended up on a "normal" trail that went along a creek bed and through beautiful pines. We then ended on the flat carriage road that overlooked the lake. Since it was getting dark, that was much better! When we got back to the beginning, we saw a couple sitting at the Pond House. They couldn't believe we went up the rocky part especially when I was in rain boots and had a dog. I just laughed. We love adventure but it was time for some HEAT! We were wet and freezing! The original plan was to stay at the campground in the park because it was cheaper, but it did not have hookups so we headed back to the campground. A hot shower and heat sounded good and well worth the extra money!

The next day we woke up to NO RAIN!! Yay!! It was still cold but we were happy to be dry, even though it hasn't been too bad hiking in the rain. I decided to take a drive down Sergeant Drive. It was a really pretty drive, and we even saw a lobster boat in action! I was eager to see what the day's hike will bring. The hikes in Acadia have not been boring!

We headed over to Eagle Lake because Ted said that Jack was allowed to swim there. It would have been a fun lake to SUP on, but even though it was warmer than the last few days, it was still pretty cold. He also suggested that we hike Beech Mountain. The trailhead was next to the lake, and we started up. It seemed like a normal hike until we got to the steel ladders! At this point, I just started laughing! Every hike I had been on had something unique about it. I had to pick Jack up and carry him up the ladders. There were four of them in total along the hike. When we got to the top of the last ladder, there was a couple from New York there enjoying the view. The woman looked at us, pointed in the other direction and told us that way was easier! It was really funny! We seem to be attracted to the challenge!

I chatted with the couple at the top for a little bit and then went down the "easier" way, Canada Cliff Trail! It was a pretty hike through the trees and streams. When we arrived at the bottom, there was a No Dogs sign for the beach. The beach was empty, so I let Jack go swimming. He was so excited! There are a lot of benefits to traveling in the off-season. I read that this park gets so crowded that you can't find parking in the parking lots, but we had most of them to ourselves! We just had to put up with a little rain and wind! I am sure that is why they don't want dogs on the beach because of the crowds so being there in the off season was another bonus, Jack got to swim!

After the swim, Jack was freezing! He will swim in ice water and stand there and shake and never want to get out!

That is where I have to be the adult and say that is enough. I wrapped him in a towel and turned the heater on in the RV to warm him up. He is so quirky! He just loves to swim no matter what!

I decided that I was ready to move on from Acadia. It has been so fun and beautiful, but it was time to go. We had been on most of the roads, did four super fun hikes, and felt that we had seen what we had come to see. But the Grand Finale was a drive up Cadillac Mountain, the highest mountain on the Atlantic Coast at 1,580 feet elevation. We had tried to go the other day, but it was so fogged in that we couldn't see anything. Luckily, today we could! I was so happy that we waited! It was beyond beautiful! The view was of all of the islands off the coast, and we got there right before sunset so that was an added bonus. We walked all around and took a ton of photos. I was wishing that we had hiked up but then we ended up sitting in the RV, eating our dinner and watching the sunset. What a great ending to a fun visit to one of the only national parks that allows dogs on the trails! Thank you, Acadia!

We headed out of Acadia feeling so much gratitude. That night we stayed in the Wal-Mart parking lot in Ellsworth. We were now a part of the Wal-Mart RV club! Most of them allow you to park in their parking lots overnight for free, which is super cool especially since I needed to stock up on groceries anyway! Plus, it was free so it made up for us staying in the pricy campground an extra night. That is how I justify things!

After our stay in Wal-Mart, we loaded up with supplies and we were on our way. We headed to Camden, Maine for a hike that Kurgo was sponsoring with the Loyal Biscuit, another small dog boutique. The drive down Route 1 was so beautiful. The sun was shining, and it was a great day! I was so happy that I waited and drove it in the daylight. We got to go through little towns, cross a really cool bridge, see tons of fishing boats and see views of the Atlantic Ocean. It was really amazing, and we highly recommend it! Jack was funny. He rode shotgun in his car seat and looked out the window like a person. I talk to him and told him where we were going. I pointed things out to him, and I swear he understood!

I really wanted to stop and take a photo of the beautiful ocean. I stopped at a RV park, but the sign at the entrance said "Private" so I turned around and went down the next driveway that led to a bunch of rental cabins. I was just about ready to take my photo when a car came flying up the road toward me. A lady put down her window and started yelling at me that I was on private property. I guess I missed the sign in this driveway. Whoops! I said that I just wanted to take a photo, but she wasn't hearing it. She wouldn't even let me go down further to turn around, she made me back the entire way up the hill. It was just part of the adventure and I never did get my photo!

We got to the Bald Rock Trailhead in Camden and pre-hiked our hike so we knew what to expect. It was a great. A mile of wide trail through beautiful Aspen and then the trail turned up a root-y and rocky side trail for about a half a mile. The view from the top was AMAZING!! This view reminded me of why we started this journey in the first place. It was a view like this on the Pacific Ocean a year ago that inspired us to hike around the country and see the beautiful views. From this view, we could see eagles flying over the trees near the coast. It was simply spectacular! We felt so blessed and took a few moments to be grateful for all that we got to see and do! I was not taking any of this for granted. I was so thankful for all of it.

After the hike, we headed into the city of Camden. We passed a lake that was screaming for Jack to swim in it, and it just so happened to have a dock. Since it was a nice day, Jack got to SWIM! I contemplated getting the SUP out, but wanted to get a few other things done that took priority.

Camden was a super cute town on the water. We walked all over the town and it was even warm enough for me to get ice cream. I love ice cream and couldn't pass up the chance to get "lobster" ice cream. It was really just a marketing ploy, there was no lobster in it but the vanilla with chocolate swirls was good anyhow. The boats on the harbor were really big and beautiful, and we saw a lot of lobster traps. We really were in Maine!

It was fun walking around the town but it was time to head to Camden Hills State Park to see where we were camping. This is one site that I booked ahead of time since we were here on a busy weekend and there didn't seem to be a lot of campgrounds in the area. I am very picky when it comes to campsites and I like to see them before I camp in them. Most of the sites in this campground were on a hill so it took me three times to find a site where we could get level. We finally decided on a site that was in the grass and close to the entrance and trails. The park rangers were super nice and they didn't care that we switched sites.

Chapter 13: Maine

Since we were across the street from the ocean, we took a walk down to the "beach" that turned out to be a rocky cliff. The waves were breaking on the rocks, and it was a really beautiful site. I decided to return at sunrise since this might be our last chance at seeing the sunrise over the Atlantic Ocean. We were sad that our journey was going to be taking us back west tomorrow. Our journey had been so much fun and we didn't want it to end!

We had to rise at 4:40 a.m. to see the sunrise. We almost missed it because Jack had to stop and poop, and I couldn't get the bag open in the dark. Don't you hate it when that happens? The sky was a beautiful pink color! Unfortunately, the sunrise was hard to see because of the fog bank that rolled in, but we got a little glimpse of it. It was very cold so we went back to the RV and went back to bed. Since it was so nice yesterday, we thought it would be warm again today but that was not the case. We won't be SUPing in the lake today!

Instead, we hiked up to Mount Megunticook from camp, which was rather convenient. There were a lot of little turnoffs to see the ocean view, but it was really foggy so the view was obscured. I realized that you really can't go wrong with any hike in Maine. They have all been rather amazing and well marked. The cool weather has been perfect hiking weather - no bugs and no humidity. We don't hike in the summer in San Diego because dogs don't do well in the heat plus there is always the chance of seeing a rattlesnake! Jack has really appreciated the cool weather. I was laughing because I was bundled up in three layers, and I saw two gals on the hike in tank tops and shorts. They were obviously locals!

I decided to get all prettied up and go on a "date night" with my boy! We were running low on propane and I wanted to buy some real blueberry jam, so we were on a mission. In addition, I thought I had better get some chowder before we departed Maine. Some things you just have to do when you are a tourist!

We took a drive down the coast and saw beautiful houses and cows grazing near the coast. They had some very expensive pasture! Four boys were filming a video in Camden and thought our journey was really cool so they took a photo by Spirit with Jack. It was fun to see even young guys were interested in what we were doing. We thought that Camden would be crowded since it was Friday night, but it was quiet. I got my chowder and then we walked down to the beach. We had to put our toes in the Atlantic Ocean to signify it was time to move west. Our mission was complete! It was a fun "date night", as you can tell from our journey, we don't get out in civilization much.

The next day, we woke to rain. I was so disappointed. It was National Trails Day and our hike with the Loyal Biscuit was going to go on no matter what! We don't mind hiking in the rain but we didn't want it to scare anyone else from joining us. We were getting good at it. We kept having crazy coincidences happen on this journey and this day was another one! Our friends from San Diego just happened to be in Maine and they joined us on the hike! They used to live in Maine and were there for a friend's party. We actually just missed them in Acadia. Cathy and Frank Hardalo are an important part of Leash Your Fitness, and I can't think of anyone that I would rather see when I am 5,000 miles away from home. Plus, Cathy makes the best treats and shares them with us! We share her recipes on our blog so others can make homemade, healthy treats for their dogs, too!

I was so excited to see my Uncle Frank and especially my Aunt Cathy. She is my most favorite California Aunty. (I had to clarify that so my Aunty Lynn wouldn't get upset) Cathy always has the most yummy treats for me every time that I see her and she is always so nice to me!

As they say in this part of the country, if you don't like the weather, wait 5 minutes. That definitely rang true. It turned out to be a beautiful morning, and the hike was super fun. A few people didn't show up because of the weather but those who did were very happy. The view from the top was just as amazing as the first time that we saw it.

It is always fun to share it with friends and see how excited they are. We like introducing people to fun activities that they can do with their dog. That is what why we are here. Now the local people know of a cool hike that they can do with their dog.

Loyal Biscuit and Kurgo had goodie bags for everyone on the hike and we got some great photos. Now we had someone that we knew in every class that we taught so far on this trip. That was pretty astonishing if you ask me!

After the hike, Cathy, Frank and I went to lunch on the water, and I had one last lobster roll before leaving Maine. The restaurant was right on the water near the ferry landing. We watched as the ferry took off to go to the islands where the rich and famous live. John Travolta and Kirstie Alley have houses on the islands there. We dipped our feet in the Atlantic Ocean one last time, said our goodbyes to our friends and headed west. I was sad to be heading toward home but excited about the rest of our trip. I didn't have anywhere planned to stay that night so I just started driving toward the White Mountains in New Hampshire. I heard that they were a fun place to hike.

We just started driving and knew we would figure it out on the way. That is what we do sometimes. We passed Liberty State Park and we thought we could stay there since it was on a beautiful lake. It was getting warm and we really wanted to SUP in Maine. However, the woman directed us to Sebago State Park that was closer to our destination, so we drove an hour and a half there. Jack was super excited to go swimming, and it seemed like the drive took forever.

We finally arrived and the guy at the gate told us the dreaded words that we hate to hear. "NO DOGS!" *WHAT?* Jack was out of control excited at this point since I had been telling him for the last two hours that we were going swimming, so I had to do something quick. I drove back down the road and found the nearest campground, Sebago Crooked River Campground. It was nice, but I wasn't sure if it would work with the iSUP. So we walked down to the river to check it out. What a beautiful river with hardly any current! PERFECT! We were sold! We paid and immediately inflated the SUP. We couldn't get on the water fast enough.

Our new neighbors were very intrigued by our RV, so they came over to see what was up. Annabelle and TJ and their dog, Duncan, ended up being super cool! They were in the Army and from the area. We ended up hanging out with them for the next two days!

They rented a kayak and we had our SUP, and we took a little paddle on the river. They had never kayaked before, so this was their maiden voyage. It was getting late so we headed back to camp - but not before they tried out the SUP! They both did really well on it even though they were nervous about falling in.

We asked them why they didn't bring Duncan on the kayak with them and their reply was typical, "He doesn't like the water." Little do people know that when their dog doesn't like the water that is even better. Dogs like Jack who LOVE the water want to jump out the entire time. When your dog doesn't like the water, he tends to sit quietly and just enjoy the ride. There is no reason for your dog to get wet unless you capsize the watercraft and then you are all getting wet. You should have a dog life jacket on your dog, especially if they don't like to swim. There was not one available at this campground, but thankfully, they didn't need it.

Our new neighbors invited us over for dinner after our water adventure. I was excited that I was able to eat real food. Most of the time when we are camping, I just graze all day. I only eat occasional meals that consist of salads, canned beans or chicken or whatever else I can throw together quickly. I am not much of a cook! I have never even used the oven in the RV. I don't even know how to turn it on!

After dinner we had s'mores with peanut butter cups! This was our first campfire and first s'more on our entire trip! Can you believe that? I am not much of a fire builder either!

I guess I should probably work on that. It was a really nice chatting with our new friends. They were really funny and had some great stories. I live in San Diego where all of the military people are in the Navy and Marines so it was cool to meet a couple that met in the Army.

The next day was BEAUTIFUL!! I was so happy to be in shorts again. I even put on my bathing suit because we were going to spend the entire day on the Crooked River paddling down to Sebago Lake that is 5 miles away. This would be our longest paddle ever and a big feat for TJ and Annabelle since this was only their second time in a kayak! After a delicious breakfast with Annabelle and TJ, we were on our way.

Annabelle and TJ decided to take Duncan this time and he did GREAT! He sat in the kayak and was such a good boy. He was just taking in the sights around him like a person would. At one point, Annabelle put her hat on his head. He was such a cool dog. I was a little jealous since Jack never just sits quiet and still when we are anywhere near water!

The paddle was so beautiful. This river is not very wide, but there were boats on it. There were also cabins and houses lining the river. We even got to go into a lock. The lock keepers took our picture for us in between letting big boats through. That was pretty cool! I grew up water skiing on the Monongahela River in Pennsylvania that had locks and big barges. One time, my sister and I were in charge of the boat while our older brother was water skiing. He kicked off a ski and was skiing solo. When he fell and we went back to get the ski, the towrope got caught in the motor. It took a while for us to get it untangled. By the time we went back for our bother, a barge had gone by. We panicked thinking our brother had been run over by the barge! Instead, he had swam to shore to wait for us. Needless to say, we were never allowed to be in charge of the boat alone again! It was fun taking a trip down memory lane and this time, paddling in a lock, it had been over 30 years since I had even seen one!

We met another couple that were paddling in kayaks, too, so they paddled down to the lake with us. It was super fun. The ironic part is the guy used to work where TJ did. It is such a small world. We chatted to each other and paddled and enjoyed the day.

We took our time and enjoyed the beautiful river. When we got to the lake, it was HUGE! The cool part was there was a sand bar so we paddled to it and got to hang out and have snacks and swim. Jack and Duncan were running up and down the sandbar having a blast! Of course, Jack was having a blast swimming. Duncan got on the SUP. He was a little nervous at first but he did really well. He just stood there while I paddled him around. We even got him to go in the water. It took a few treats at first, but then Annabelle went in. He swam right to her, and they were playing in the water!

It was a day of firsts for him. It was a good reminder never to underestimate your dog. You never know what they will do if you give them the chance. Duncan was a bait dog and had the scars to prove it. You would never know that was in Duncan's past. He was a real sweetheart and a lot of fun. We were so happy that he ended up in a good home with Annabelle and TJ. They love him a lot, and they make a really nice family.

A bait dog is used in dogfights. They use them to give the dogs practice on being mean and attacking. They usually get rescued when they are no longer needed by the fighters or else they are dumped somewhere to die. Sometimes authorities break up the outfit that is putting on the fights and all of the dogs get rescued. Rescue organizations spend a lot of time rehabbing the dogs so they are safe to be around people. Some can be rehabbed and unfortunately some have to be put down. It is a very sad situation but, unfortunately, it goes on everywhere. Dogs like Duncan prove that the dogs can be rehabbed, be really nice dogs that just want to be loved.

After our break on the sand bar, we headed back to camp. On the paddle down to the lake, I was telling Annabelle about all of the amazing things that kept happening to us. Even finding this campground when the other one didn't allow dogs turned out to be a blessing! So Annabelle asked if we could use our "powers" to get a motor to take her back to camp on the way back. This was only their second time paddling. They were doing well, but they were getting tired.

I used my "powers" to help her. Our camp neighbor, Jane, who we had just met that morning at breakfast, came by on her pontoon boat. TJ and Annabelle were a little ahead of Jack and I at this point, so I asked Jane if she could tow them back. She happily agreed. She caught up with them and they tethered their kayaks onto her pontoon and were towed back to camp. It was so cool and Annabelle couldn't believe it! Our travel spirits helped us in so many amazing ways.

I paddled back, and we stopped a few times to go swimming. The water was cold, but it felt really good. It was a gorgeous day. It started to cloud up with a threat of rain, and a boat stopped and offered us a ride back. We thanked them but declined, taking the chance that the rain would pass us by. It did! It is so refreshing to see how nice people are everywhere that we go.

We got back to camp and Annabelle and TJ had a late lunch ready for me. They were spoiling me, and I knew I was going to miss them. It was so fun to meet them and we were excited for their future together as they will be getting married next year.

After they packed up and left, I took a hot shower at the campground. I had never seen such a pretty shower room at a campground. It was really clean. I did laundry, too, and the laundry room was nice as well. It had a sitting room with a table so I could get some work done on my laptop while doing laundry. Of course, Jack goes everywhere with me so he took a little nap while I worked.

The other good thing was that it had grass. Most of the sites that we stayed at were dirt or mud because of the rain, so it was nice to be able to get a few things out of the RV and clean it a little. We scored when we found this campground, and I would highly recommend it.

The next day we woke to a cloudy morning – perfect for me to lounge around and read. I love mornings like this! I even took my yoga mat out in the grass and did some yoga and some foam rolling. It was Monday and most of the campers left, so we practically had the entire campground to ourselves. With a charged laptop, empty tanks and my back and legs all stretched out, it was time to head out to our next destination. We were going to continue our journey to the White Mountains.

When traveling, I would highly recommend you stretch. Sitting for prolonged periods of time is not good for your back. Your hip muscles get tight and that in turn pulls on your back. I stretch regularly and use a foam roller to roll out my legs. You can purchase them in most sporting good stores. I roll my legs on it to get out any 'knots' that are causing my muscles to get tight. I also roll out my upper and lower back. It feels like I am getting a massage!

Chapter 14: New Hampshire

T
he drive to the White Mountains was short from the Crooked River Campground. We stopped at the Ranger Station on the Kancamagus Highway (Route112) and asked the ranger where we should hike. It was already 2 p.m. and a cloudy day with threatening rain. He suggested the Chamney Falls hike. I heard waterfalls, so we were on our way. I love waterfalls! We stopped at a few view spots along the way and then headed up the trail.

The two-mile trail was scenic along a stream most of the way. We were so excited when we got to the first waterfall, and then we kept going and they kept getting better! We even hiked through the stream a little. Jack was a little confused as to whether he should go in the water or not because it was super COLD! We hung out at the waterfall long enough for the view to clear, and we took a good photo of the mountains. I'm not sure which peak it was, but it was beautiful! We only saw one other person on the hike and he was a native to the area. He told me that this was his favorite hike in the area so that made me feel better because the weather wasn't cooperating to do any more hikes there. I don't like to miss anything!

I don't mind cold water but sometimes when the creek bed is full of river rocks and the water is really cold, it hurts my paws. Mommy knows this so she sometimes carries me or hikes around the creek.

After our short hike, we drove up the road and stopped at a few more stops along the way. We saw another waterfall. The fog occluded the views and that was a bummer, so we missed a lot of the beautiful scenery. We were going to spend the night in the campground there but since it was kind of rainy and we couldn't see anything because of the fog, we decided to keep driving. We were headed back to our friend, Kelli's house in New York. If we started to head that way that night, our drive would be shorter the next day.

I don't really like driving at night so when it started getting dark, I began looking for places that we could stay for the night. In the past, I had always found a rest stop, truck stop or Wal-Mart that worked for a safe place to just park and sleep. I have a few apps on my phone and none of those were options in this area, so I just kept driving. Route 202 was a nice road but there wasn't much on it. When you are traveling alone, it is sometimes hard to navigate while you are driving. I was getting tired, and I didn't want to spend the money on a campground just to sleep. So, we turned the night into another adventure.

I finally saw a gas station off one of the exits. I asked the gal who was working if we could spend the night in the back parking lot. She didn't see why not, so we ended up staying the night in the back lot of a gas station along the road. It was weird. We pulled around the back and there was a perfect pullout for us in the corner. It was like it was put there just for Spirit! I was a little nervous because the gas station was closing at 11 p.m., but she assured us that the police cruised through the area and that it was a very safe neighborhood. I must have not been too concerned because I fell asleep and slept until 6:30 a.m. That is late for me! That morning, workers were giving me strange looks. I don't think they knew what I was doing there. I thanked them, and we were off to Kelli's house again! We were about to do a little backtracking now on our journey.

Since it was on our way to Michigan, we were going back to teach another class for Studio 8 Fitness in New York with our friend, Kelli, and then head to Chautauqua to visit my sister, Lynn, again. This time, her boat was ready for us. I was excited to see Jack on the boat and jet ski! He has only ever been on one boat before and never on a jet ski.

On the way to Kelli's house, I saw a bunch of places that we could have pulled in and slept last night, but it worked out and plus the drive was prettier during the day. We took the country roads through the little New Hampshire and Vermont towns. It was my boyfriend's birthday and he loves maple syrup, so we stopped at a place in Vermont to get him some REAL Maple Syrup. That ended up being the best gift that I could have ever given to him. He loved it! We stopped near a lake so that Jack could get a swim. I have my priorities! I caught up on my journaling looking over the beautiful lake. It was nice to get a break from driving, and we took advantage of all of the beautiful fresh water lakes. We don't have these in San Diego! It has been such a spiritual and fulfilling journey so far, and there is more to come!

Chapter 15: New York Again

We got to Kelli's house in New Hartford, NY. It was raining, but we didn't care. I think I have been in more rain on this trip than I have experienced in the last 20 years in San Diego. Because of that, it's pretty cool for us. We had another dog fitness class there scheduled with her friends from Studio 8. A few weren't able to come last time so they were excited to try it out. We held class in the rain. It was so fun. We ran around and did some drills and when it started pouring, we took class under the covering, and I showed them exercises to do on the tables. There are a lot of exercises that you can do with the tables like pushups, step-ups, dips, one-legged lunges and many more. Kelli's clients were the nicest people ever, and we really appreciated them coming out to see us again, especially in the rain!

After class, it was nice to spend more time with Kelli and her family. She and her daughters prepared a delicious and healthy fish dinner for me. I was definitely getting spoiled on this trip! Traveling has its perks. Sadly, Jack was not a very nice guest. He would not play with Cody. Cody kept trying so hard to get Jack to play, but Jack was being a bully. He is not a fan of puppies, and he isn't really a "play with other dogs" kind of dog. Poor Cody. Instead, Kelli's daughter showed me the tricks she taught Cody. She was doing a great job training him.

Teaching your dogs tricks is a great way to mentally stimulate him. Most dogs love to please you and entertain. Start with what your dog already does and turn it into a 'trick'. For example, if your dog does the upward dog stretch every morning, call it "stretch" every time he does it and give him a treat. Pretty soon, he will do it on cue!

To Kelli's dismay, I spent the night in the driveway in the RV. It was plenty warm, and I was planning on rising early and getting on the road by 5 a.m. to my sister's house. After all, it was going to be another four-hour drive and I wanted to get there early so we could spend the day playing on the water. I took the toll road to save time. Driving in New York was expensive, especially in a RV. It cost more than $20 in tolls just to get there plus the gas in New York was very expensive. Today was the third drive day in a row so when I arrived at Lynn's house, I decided to spend a few days there. I needed a break from driving. Plus, I could use the time to clean the RV, wash my clothes, get caught up with my blog and, of course, spend more time with my family.

I arrived to a sunny and warm day – perfect for the lake. Jack was so excited to go swimming again and dock diving. He loved it there. There were a lot of squirrels he could chase. It was a nice walk from Lynn's house to where her boat was docked. Since it was a weekday, there was hardly anyone at home, so Jack was having a blast running around the never-ending yards. There were no fences and where my sister lives, it was a dead end road. The only cars were the people who live there, so Jack was just having a blast running around. It was so fun seeing him have so much fun!

I got to run down the dock as fast as I could and then when mommy gave the okay, I would dock dive into the water and then swim to shore, run through the grass, back up on the dock and do it again and again and again! Then I even got to ride on the jet ski! How many dogs can say that they did that? That is what Jack's Journey USA is all about, trying new things and inspiring others to do new activities with their dog! Then Aunt Lynn took us out in the boat, and I got to jump off of the boat into the water! It was the best day ever.

To say that he was excited was an understatement. My dream is to live on a lake in an area that doesn't get cold in the winter! Any suggestions? That is Jack's dream, too!

We took the boat over to a restaurant on the lake. It had plenty of outdoor seating and since it was a weekday, we had the entire restaurant to ourselves. In San Diego, many restaurants allow dogs on their outdoor patios, so I just assumed it was that way everywhere. That was not the case! They didn't allow dogs on the patio, but the nice people in the restaurant made an exception for Jack. He is very well behaved and just laid by the table while we enjoyed lunch, overlooking the lake. It might have helped that there weren't any other customers there.

> **The people at the restaurant asked if Jack was a service dog. I do not lie and say that he is. I feel that is a disservice to the people who really need service dogs. It is also bad Karma. Service dogs come in all breeds. They are specifically trained dogs who do not act out in public and are very well behaved and well trained.**

It was a fun and relaxing day. It was nice to know that we still had one more day to hang out here and not have to drive. It would be nice to have four more days here, but we are happy with one. It was good to hang out on the boat, chat with my family and just enjoy the beauty of the lake. My niece, Laura, was here this time and Jack loves her as do I so I was so happy that we came back to spend time with her. She is the niece who drove across country with me the last time that I made this journey over 5 years ago. She had just turned 17 and I allowed her to drive my SUV the entire way. She is very responsible and did a super job. This time, we had fun racing around together on the jet ski! Jack got to have his first ride on the jet ski. I held him and we went very slow. He didn't know what to think of it. All he wanted to do was jump into the water. But now he can add that to his resume of activities that he has done.

The next morning, the lake was super calm so Lynn, Jack and I went SUPing. The last time that we were here a few weeks ago, Lynn tried my SUP. She loved it so much that she ordered one. Now it was perfect! We all got to go together, and we paddled down to the Chautauqua Bell Tower. It was a nice paddle. The water was super calm in the mornings and there were not many boats out. It was good practice for my sister on her new iSUP, too!

The day turned out to be beautiful so we spent the entire day on the lake. Laura came with us in the boat, and Jack got to swim and swim and swim! The Chautauqua Institute was still not in season yet so we docked the boat and went on a little tour of Chautauqua. It was a nice walk around the grounds. We stopped in a few stores and I got a Bell Tower tree ornament. I collect tree ornaments from my travels so every Christmas it is fun to decorate the tree and reminisce about my travels. The buildings there were so old and big! We got some photos taken at the huge hotel that was right on the lake. It was a beautiful hotel. The lobby was enormous and the front deck was lined with rocking chairs that overlooked the lake. It would have been a nice place to relax and read if you were staying there.

Jack was so tired on the boat ride home that he fell asleep in Laura's arms. It was so cute. He never used to allow anyone to touch him, so when someone gets to hold him and pet him, it is a big deal. Over the years, he has become more trusting, and he allows a select few to give him love. When I got Jack, he was the puppy in the back corner. Some people base their puppy on looks, I based mine on his temperament. The other puppies were barking and jumping up, he was sitting quietly in the back. He wasn't abused; he just didn't ever like to be touched. It drove everyone crazy because he was so cute, and he wouldn't allow anyone to pet or hold him. I even had my boyfriend feed him every day, and it took a long time for Jack to even allow Jim to hold him. I don't think it is a trust issue. Jack just doesn't like to be touched. He is very independent.

It is just his personality, and I have grown to accept it.

Spirit was shiny clean as were all of my clothes. My sister loaded me up with fresh baked cookies and Jack and I were off again. We were both sad to leave Chautauqua, but we were excited to visit a new state. Michigan will be his 32nd state and the 10th new one on this journey. We get to stay in Michigan for an entire week!

Chapter 16: Michigan

It is always sad for me to leave my family as I don't see them often and never know the next time we can get together. This journey made it possible to visit WITH Jack. We had such a fun time in Lake Chautauqua just like I knew that we would. The weather was great to get out on the lake. I feel so fortunate that the weather has cooperated with us on this trip. I am just hoping that the good weather gods will follow us to Michigan!

Jack swam in all 31 states, and he planned to swim in Michigan, too! We were really excited to venture into this state. I have wanted to visit Michigan for a long time!

Jack was so tired that he slept on the entire ride to Michigan. I decided to forgo the tolls and take the more scenic route on Route 2 in Ohio. It was pretty. We passed lots of water and even the Cedar Point Amusement Park. I used to go there as a kid. When the GPS says 6.5 hours, we always tack on a few hours for various stops, traffic and so forth. We arrived at Indian Valley Campground nine hours later. We stopped to load up on groceries and found a Costco to get some gas.

Indian Valley Campground is south of Grand Rapids. Once again, we took a bunch of back roads to get to it. It is always a mystery where the campground is going to be, and that is part of the fun.

Once we arrived, we had the site that we booked moved so that we were on the river. That is why I don't like booking sites ahead of time. You never know what they look like. We didn't have a choice in campgrounds. A lot of the nearby campgrounds were booked solid because of a big music festival going on, so I didn't want to take any chances of not getting a site since we had to teach in Grand Rapids the following day. Plus, they were very accommodating here.

It didn't take Jack long to be out of the RV and swimming, especially after nine hours in the RV. Our new neighbor, Emily, was very well versed in dogs. She had a lot of stories for us about her rescues. The one that she currently had was a pug/ Lhasa apso mix – a crazy looking dog! Her boyfriend, Eli, had a husky who pulled him on his skateboard. That dog was in his element while pulling Eli. We scored having them as neighbors. It was so fun to meet such cool, dog-loving people everywhere we go!

It felt like a welcoming little community at this campground. Many live there full time. A huge family pulled in next to me. They were super nice and loved Jack. They sat around, played guitar, and partied, but I had to get up early to teach, so I was a party pooper. I went to bed early and missed all of the fun.

The next morning, we went to Knox Park near Allegro Coaching in Grand Rapids to teach our Leash Your Fitness class. I landed this location because Kendra Bylsma, the owner of Allegro, used to be in my Mastermind Group. When I was planning the trip and wanted to go to Michigan, I contacted her. Kendra loves dogs and she was all for me teaching a class for her members. It was a fundraiser for the Bissell Foundation. They raise money to help shelters around the country. How cool is that? That was a shock to me that a vacuum cleaner company did that. We helped raise $350 in our Leash Your Fitness class. We were so happy that it went to dogs in need.

Again, it was threatening rain, but the weather gods held out, and we had perfect weather! The class was our largest yet. There were over 30 dogs! We had dogs of all sizes, including an English Bulldog named Brutus!

I went over a bunch of drills, we did a little agility and ended with doggy yoga. We went into the vacant, fenced tennis court and did some obedience drills with the dogs. They were told to stay and their parents had to exercise around them. It was fenced in, so they were safe and they weren't going anywhere. The dogs did great, plus we showed the parents some new drills for them to do with their dogs. The 90 minutes flew by and the dogs were all good and tired at the end! That is our goal because a tired dog is a happy dog!

It was fun visiting with Kendra. She is super busy. She has a newborn boy, a little girl and was in the middle of building a new house while running her business. I was thrilled that she took the time to have breakfast with me after class. I got to visit her studio that she had just expanded. It looked like a really fun place to workout. The area around her fitness facility was really cool. We went to a healthy breakfast place and chatted about everything. It had been a few years since

I had seen her so it was a short, but productive few hours of catching up. I enjoyed our morning together. I really appreciated that she had me come to teach there. It worked out perfectly.

After class, the sun came out, and it ended up being a beautiful day! We drove over to Lake Michigan and explored a little of the shoreline. It was beautiful. The beaches were white sand, and the water was so blue, it looked like the Caribbean. I never knew Lake Michigan was so big. We found an empty beach that went on for miles. It was a bummer that the dogs weren't allowed on the beaches. They were completely empty (we are so spoiled in San Diego). We then went into Holland. It was a cute little town with a lot of windmills. I wasn't really in the touristy mood, but it was fun looking around.

It was getting warm. What we really wanted to do was inflate the SUP and go swimming, so we headed back to camp. I paddled a few miles on the river. It was a little muddy, but Jack didn't mind. Once again, we had the entire river to ourselves.

When we got back to camp, we inspired all of our new friends to try the iSUP. A few of them didn't think that they could do it, but I convinced them that they could. They all did GREAT. A few of them were even drinking alcohol and still maintained their balance without falling in. That was a good thing since they were in their street clothes. Although it would have made for a good story if they would have fell in! Lucky for them, the iSUP is pretty darn stable.

It was super fun to inspire people all day long. First, we showed the class fun drills that they can add into their dogs' daily routine to improve their behaviors. Then we introduced a new activity for our friends at camp. Many of them live near beautiful lakes and now they feel confident that they can SUP.

The next day we woke to *pouring* rain that continued all morning long. Our camp was a mess, plus we had a leak in Spirit. I couldn't figure out where the leak was coming from under the floor mat in the front so once again, it was soaked. I hadn't brought in any of the towels or the iSUP, so I spent the morning getting soaked while I brought all of that into Spirit. I reminded myself that it was all part of the adventure, and after all, it was only water (and mud!). I spent a few hours working in the RV before we headed out to our next stop. We were heading north toward Traverse City, MI where we hear it is super beautiful!

Thanks to Emily at the Indian Valley Campground, we stopped at Croton Dam Campground on the way to Traverse City. We are going to Traverse City to teach a dog fitness class with Woofers on the Run. Val Dietz, the owner, contacted us two weeks ago. She read about our trip, saw that we were going to be in Grand Rapids and asked if we could come to Traverse City to teach a class for her. Once again, everything worked out. The same week that our Ohio stop cancelled on us, Traverse City called! We just happened to have extra time and heard it is beautiful there. It sounds like a win-win, so I said YES! She was surprised and excited. She didn't know if she would have enough time to market the class, but she said she would do the best that she could. She even hooked us up with a place to stay. Her friend, Sally, said we could park Spirit in her driveway that overlooks a lake. How could we turn that down?

It was super rainy when we left Grand Rapids and we had a few days before we needed to be in Traverse City, so I thought it would be fun to just go somewhere and hang out by the water and read my book and relax. We scored big time. We got a site ON the water with a dock, and it was super cheap with hookups!

I set up camp and Jack was dock diving in no time! I just wanted to read my book, and it was a little chilly for me, so Jack made friends with the neighbor girls and they played in the water with him. It was really cute and fun to watch. They were throwing the ball for him and then they would jump in and swim with him. He won't let them touch him, but he loved it when the kids threw the ball for him. It was nice just hanging out at the campsite. The view was gorgeous and relaxing. It was an early night for me. One thing about being so far north, it gets dark really late. I am embarrassed to say that some nights I went to bed before the sunset!

The next day, the sun was out. We were so happy! We inflated the iSUP and paddled around the lake. It was really big even though the lady we had met kayaking called it a pond. It was certainly the biggest pond I had ever seen! Obviously, she had never been to California to see what we have there. The lake even had a little island on it with a house and a dock. It was really cute. The lady said it was the party house. I can see why. It was out in the middle of the lake and the island was so small that there was only room for the little house, an outhouse and a little land to party on! I thought what a cool place to spend the weekend. Jack was so happy. He jumped off the dock a few times and swam a lot. I was in no hurry, so we were just hanging out in the middle of the lake relaxing.

Chapter 16: Michigan

It got cloudy so we headed back to camp so I could finish my book. I really love to read. I do not watch TV, so reading is my "get away" time. I really like historical fiction so that I can learn about history a little while enjoying the story. I also love books about dogs. In our Leash Your Fitness business in San Diego, we even have a book club. All of the books that we read are about dogs. The only criteria is that the dog doesn't die at the end. I have even had the authors come to our book club or Skype in to discuss the book with our gals. They love it and we have learned a lot.

While I was reading, Jack had fun chasing squirrels. It was Monday morning, and it is still not tourist season yet even though it is June. The park is mostly vacant except for the people who live here. I am finding that in almost every campground, there are people who live year round. I wonder if I could live in Spirit? I think about it often! What would it be like to just travel around and live in trailer parks? There are definitely some that are nicer than others, but the commonality is that most campers are super nice! I think it would be fun.

It rained a little, but it was nice to sit under the awning and enjoy it. Jack, of course, laid out in the middle of the mud while it was raining! The boy clearly loves water! Most of the dogs in San Diego won't even go out to potty when it rains. Not Jack! He says "Bring it ON!" When we do our yearly Leash Your Fitness camping trip, Jack is the only one running around "naked." All of the other dogs have on sweaters or some sort of clothes to keep them warm during the cool nights. Jack doesn't want to be bothered. He doesn't even like it when you cover him up with a blanket. He is my little tough guy.

After it rained, we went back out on the lake in the other direction this time. We noticed that there were a lot of swans on this lake. I am not sure why. They are really pretty and so fun to watch. It almost seemed like they would let you get near them, but then they swam away quickly as soon as you headed in their direction. This lake was HUGE, and there were a lot of really nice houses on the water. Lucky for them!

We got back from the paddle just in the knick of time. It poured down rain and never stopped all night long! We don't hear rain like that in San Diego – that is for sure! This time, I got the iSUP rolled up before the rain hit and put the towels under the awning. I was learning! My sister told me about an app for the phone called "Dark Sky's." It is pretty accurate on how soon the rain will come and stop. Although it didn't warn me for this storm. It said light drizzle but this was heavy rain!

The next morning was beautiful. I dried off the awning, took a hot shower in the shower room and we packed up. We were headed to Sleeping Bear Dunes National Park – another dog-friendly national park. According to their website, Sleeping Bear Dunes National Park was named the "Most Beautiful Place in America" On ABC's Good Morning America. I was excited to see it!

The trails were fun, but the park was very crowded. It must FINALLY be tourist season! It was the first real tourist place that we have been when the tourists were actually there. It is the middle of June now so we will have to expect it for the rest of our trip. Traveling in the non-tourist season was so much easier. We didn't have to make reservations, plenty of parking everywhere we went and we had everything to ourselves. It was just funny answering all of the questions about our trip. Spirit was bright yellow with Jack's photo all over it, plus our sponsors' information, so we were getting a variety of funny questions all day. One guy asked if we were a bakery because on the door is says "Powered by One Dog Organic Bakery." Another guy asked us if we had a film crew following us because it says, "As seen on Animal Planet" on the side. The day was full of questions at every stop but I didn't mind. It was an ice-breaker and a chance to tell people about our journey.

We drove on the Scenic Loop. It was pretty crowded at most of the stops. Dogs were allowed on the Cottonwood trail. We walked to the end of it and down the dunes a little. It was a little confusing because this trail hooked into the trail that dogs were not allowed so I am not sure where one ended and the other started. I think that they did not want dogs out far on the sand dunes. We explored the dunes a little, but they went on forever. You could eventually walk out to see the lake but it was a really far walk. It started getting warm, so we turned around.

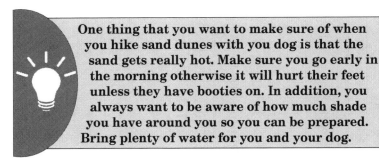

One thing that you want to make sure of when you hike sand dunes with you dog is that the sand gets really hot. Make sure you go early in the morning otherwise it will hurt their feet unless they have booties on. In addition, you always want to be aware of how much shade you have around you so you can be prepared. Bring plenty of water for you and your dog.

After we were done exploring, we drove a little further to the Lake Michigan overlook. There were many people at this stop! The view was breathtaking! The water was so blue! We walked out to the edge to get a photo and I noticed that people were climbing down the steep dune to the water so we thought, "What the heck! We will go too!" Of course, Jack was the only dog on the dune. I am not even sure if he was allowed. Technically, I don't think anyone is really allowed to run down the dunes, but there were tons of people doing it.

Man, it was steep! The lake at the bottom was worth it, though! A few of the people watching said it was going to take hours to get back up, but I timed us. It only took us 15 minutes to climb back to the top. It was a great leg workout. Jack's little legs did great in the deep sand.

Here comes the crazy part! We were half way up the steep dune and a man said to me, "Is that your RV out on the road?" At this point, I was so used to people asking me crazy questions that I was waiting to hear what he was going to ask me.

I said, "Yes, it is."

He said, "I think you are staying at our house tonight!"

Can you believe that? The people whose house we were staying at were climbing the dunes at the same time we were! We met Sally and her entire family in the middle of a giant sand dune over an hour away from their house! Crazy good things kept happening to us, and I loved it! I chatted with them for a few minutes and told them that I would be seeing them soon!

Chapter 16: Michigan

We made one more stop before we went to Traverse City and that was to Glen Haven so Jack could swim. Is he spoiled or what? I took a walk down the beach. It was so peaceful. The people on the beach got a kick out of how much fun Jack was having and I was thrilled that he was allowed to be there. After he had his fun, I stopped in Glen Arbor for ice cream. I had to screech to a stop when I saw the ice cream shop and then fit Spirit into this little parking area. Everyone at the ice cream shop was watching me. It turns out we saw some people that we met earlier in the day enjoying their ice cream. It was fun being a tourist – we all went to the same spots!

We arrived in Traverse City and went straight to Sally's house. It was beautiful! She had a lot of water toys and a dock. Jack was in heaven! It was fun to finally meet Val after all of our correspondence setting up my stay and our class in the last few weeks. I felt like I already knew her. She and her friends welcomed Jack and I with open arms. It was so nice. I got to take a shower in Sally's house and then we were off to dinner via Sally's boat! How cool is that?

This was the first time leaving Jack in the RV alone on the trip. He was tired so that helped. We were parked in Sally's driveway so he was safe, but he does not like to miss anything, so I was just hoping that he didn't bark.

I enjoyed spending time with my new friends. We docked the boat at the restaurant and had a delicious meal. I don't eat out at restaurants much, so it was a treat. Heck, I usually wear athletic gear, so dressing in normal clothes was a treat, too! After dinner, Sally took us for a tour of the lake. It wasn't big, but it was really pretty. The park where our class is going to be was right on the lake. I already had a ton of ideas for class. We watched the sunset from the boat. It was beautiful. We were approaching the longest day of the year, and the sunset was really late in Michigan!

The next day was magnificent! Sally's house was really close to the town via a trail or via the lake. It was super convenient and a great place to stay! Jack and I paddled over to the park where we were going to have class. It was going to be fun having class on the water. I checked out the park and planned out what we could do. Every class that I have taught on this trip has been a different environment. From dog boarding facilities to trails to parks on the water, I can make anything work!

Sally was nice enough to allow us to use her washer/dryer, so I got all of my wet towels washed and dried as well as all of my other clothes. Once again, I am all caught up! I even sat on her beautiful patio overlooking the lake and got some work done. What a great morning!

I had been told that we should also go check out the Old Mission Peninsula while we were here. We lucked out and had a beautiful day for it. There was a nice trail there and an awesome beach. I didn't know that there was an official trail system there so Jack and I were bushwhacking down on the beach. Finally, I decided to walk up a little hill to see what was up there and there was a complete trail system. It was shaded and well marked. We had the best of both worlds. Jack got to hike and swim. We would highly recommend checking it out if you are ever there! The trails are behind the lighthouse.

Chapter 16: Michigan

The lighthouse sits on the 45th parallel, which means we were half way between the North and the South Poles. How often can you say that? As my brother would say, "I was jazzed". The drive home along the coast on the lake was so awesome. There were white sand beaches and beautiful homes with breathtaking views! It was a great introduction to the area. I was wondering if I could live there but then I remembered about their winters and decided, probably not!

We had a nice dinner at the West Bay Beach, a Holiday Inn resort, in the town of Traverse City that night on the water with Val. She didn't know if the restaurant would allow dogs, but they didn't say anything. I didn't see why they wouldn't allow dogs but the rules are different everywhere. Val took us for a drive around the City to see all of the large Victorian houses. They even had a brick street!

The next day, Jack and I were on the radio! It was a good interview explaining why it is important to do different activities with your dog. Make your dog think while you are spending time with him / her, and give your dog some credit. He / she wants to please you. You just have to work with them a little, just like a kid! Everyone in the radio station loved Jack and they even had treats for him. It was really fun and we were grateful that Val set it up for us. We have been on the news tons of times but it was only the second time we have been in a radio studio. Our friends in San Diego, Jagger and Kristie, are radio personalities and they had us on when we were putting on our World's Largest Dog Yoga class in January. We had 250 dogs in class and their dog, Bodie, was one of them!

Val showed us around Traverse City. They are known for their cherries so, of course, I had to have cherry ice cream! I like to eat what the natives do, plus it was another excuse to have ice cream. I also bought a bunch of weird cherry stuff, like salsa, jelly, etc. We had lunch with all of Val's friends in a former insane hospital called, The Village at Grand Traverse Commons. It was really big! It had been converted into shops, restaurants and offices and was dog friendly. We even got a chance to meet the developer as he was working in the area. Val introduced him to us. He said he wanted to make sure the entire property was dog friendly. Cool guy! After lunch, we walked around and looked at all of the stores. They were housed in the former patient rooms. Some had bars on the doors. It was a really unique place. On the walls were historical photos of what the building used to look like. They did a great job of transforming it.

The class at the park was in the evening. It was threatening rain, but I did my sun dance and called our weather gods again. It worked! The sun came out, and it was a beautiful night! We had the largest turnout of any class yet with only 2 weeks notice! Thirty-two people and dogs showed up! This was the first class on my entire journey that I did not know anyone in. I had just met Val and her friends, but other than that, I didn't know anyone. Everyone was super nice and enthusiastic. This crowd made you feel like they had known you for years! What a cool park, too! For part of the class, we got to work out on the dock on the water! We were doing wall sits on the pylons. Everyone had a great time, and they hoped that Val, from Woofers on the Run, started classes like these in Traverse City!

After class, Sally and I did a demo on how to SUP with your dog. A few people got on the SUPs and tried them, but most watched from the dock. They were intrigued and excited to try it with their dogs! After everything was done, a bunch of us went to a dog- friendly place right next to the park. It was perfect and had really good food.

Traverse City ROCKED! It was a last minute add-on to our schedule, but one of the most fun stops on the entire journey! Everyone was so nice to us, and there were so many fun things to do there. This was one stop where I would have loved to stay longer, but we couldn't since we are on a tight schedule.

We were now off to Kentucky to teach a dog yoga class with B-Fit Personal Training. We don't have long to get there, so we are going to drive straight through. It is a dog yoga class on the water!

Michigan was a fun state. Everyone was so nice to us. I loved all of the water. Everywhere we went had water! I was wondering if mommy would bring me back here again, maybe in the winter? Because I like snow too!

Chapter 17: Kentucky

We just stayed in the RV during our entire visit in Traverse City. It is just easier because everything is in there. Plus, it was plenty warm enough. So we didn't disturb anyone when we got an early start south. We knew we had long drive ahead of us. We were so happy that Val, from Woofers on the Run, called us, and we added this stop on last minute! We were really sad to leave but we don't like to wear out our welcome.

It was a long drive day. We stopped for food and gas a few times. At one of the stops for gas, the guy behind us was from Escondido, CA, 20 minutes from where we live! It is such a small world! I also stopped in Indiana at a lake to let Jack out to swim. I am such a good mommy, and he is such a good little traveler, and I needed a break from driving. Our travel time was 11 hours today, the second longest travel day on our trip! I really don't like driving that long but we didn't have a choice so I am happy that everything went as planned!

We arrived at Elizabethtown Crossroads Campground at 7 p.m. It was HOT and HUMID! The campground was okay. The sites were pretty close together, but we weren't spending much time there, so I was okay with it. Besides, we didn't have any choice. It was the only campground in the area.

After traveling for 11 hours, we both needed a little workout! I hooked up my TRX on the playground set and worked out while Jack chased his toy and squirrels. I could not believe how humid it was at 7:30 p.m.! I am not sure what was worse, the humidity or the mosquitos. I swatted mosquitos in between sets. It was pretty miserable, but at least we were here safe and out playing. We played around outside until it started pouring. It rained for 12 hours straight. I was so thankful it wasn't raining like this when I was driving.

I had to go outside and hook up the RV in the rain. I looked "sexy" in my rain boots and shorts. I think I embarrassed Jack! I was getting used to the rain! It was actually a fun break from the weather in San Diego. I had full hookups so I took a shower in the RV. I did some stretches and just read and relaxed the rest of the evening.

The next morning, we headed over to B-Fit Personal Training because they are hosting our dog yoga class here in Kentucky. It was fun seeing our friend, Beverly Johnson, and her friends and clients. It has been so delightful visiting our friends on the trip and seeing their fitness studios. We hear about them, but now we know what they are talking about! Bev is also in my Fitness Mastermind Group. I was excited when she agreed to host a class for us.

She took us to Sam Russell Provisions as they are co-sponsoring the class. It was a cool store and dog-boarding place. It looked like a house. The owner said that when they opened, nobody knew what dog boarding was, and now they had to expand because they were so busy. Dog businesses are the up and coming thing because people love their dogs! It is good to see it is happening everywhere, not just in California. When I started my Leash Your Fitness business six years ago, nobody knew what I was talking about. Now, they are starting to pop up here and there and in the media. We have been in many national magazines and TV shows and CNN, Animal Planet and the Wall Street Journal, have featured us as well as our local media outlets. We are just lucky in San Diego because we have the nice weather to be able to exercise outside year round.

Next, we went to see the park where the class was going to be. Man, it was big! The best part was that it is on a lake. It was really hot, so we would be swimming, for sure, after class. It was a cloudy and windy day, but we took the iSUP out anyhow. It was a great workout, paddling against the wind.

Man! I have never seen mommy paddle so hard. It was really windy in Kentucky. If mommy stopped paddling, we went the wrong way. I didn't dare ask her to go in swimming or we would have floated away!

When we arrived in Elizabethtown, we noticed that the play in town was "The Wizard of Oz" but guess who they were missing in their display—TOTO! So, I had to fix it and get a photo of Jack with Dorothy since Toto was a Cairn terrier like Jack. I was practicing for when we visit the Wizard of OZ museum in Kansas next week!

Sunday came and it was a beautiful day but very hot. It just so happened to be International Yoga Day so I decided to do two yoga classes that day! I went to B- Fit and took a yoga class with Jennifer. She was a good teacher, and it was fun taking someone else's class for a change. The two people who were in the class with me came to our dog yoga class, too.

Our dog yoga class was scheduled for 1 p.m., so we went early to find shade at the park. It was going to be really hot for the dogs. I wanted to be set up and have the iSUP ready for after class so everyone could try it out. It was a very pretty setting for class. Everyone got to work on their balance. A few people were surprised to find out how unbalanced they were. I was surprised how well the dogs tolerated the heat. I guess it is what they were used to. Our California dogs would have been worthless in this heat!

It was Father's Day, so we were happy to celebrate the dads in the class. It was nice to have guys doing a yoga class. Men need to stretch, too!

Jack even found a girlfriend in class. Stormie was a Westie who looked just like him except she was white She even loved to SUP and swim! Too bad we don't live here or we could hang out more often! She was very cute and really well behaved in class.

Kim Flatley and her pup, Oscar, came the whole way from St Louis, Missouri to take the class. She will be starting classes there soon. Her business is called, Fitness With Fido. I was impressed with her dedication and disappointed that we did not set up a class in St Louis, especially since I am driving straight through there. That would have been a great kick off for her business. She and her boyfriend really liked the class, and I was excited to meet them both.

After class, everyone tried the iSUP and loved it. It was fun to see the dogs on the board for the first time! A few people even went out more than once and each time their dogs got better and more relaxed on the board.

After everyone left, I decided it would be better to get on the road that night and beat the Monday traffic through Louisville. I hadn't reserved another night at the campground so w e took off toward Illinois. We got through Louisville with no problem and headed west. We ended up staying in a rest stop with our trucker friends. It was an interesting night.

Chapter 18: Illinois

We ended up leaving Elizabethtown around 5 p.m. for our next stop. We weren't exactly sure where it was going to be so we just started driving west. We ended up staying in a rest stop in Indiana because I didn't feel like driving anymore. It was getting dark and there was a storm brewing. It was a nice rest stop. It even had an attendant, so I felt very safe. He showed us the best place to park, and it was perfect because I got awesome photos of the lightening show! It was nice sleeping during the pouring rain.

It was funny when we woke up the next morning. I was parked at the end of this long row of semi-trucks, and it made Spirit looked so tiny! I was really happy that we stayed there.

We left early in the morning to go to Wayne Fitzgerrell State Park on Rend Lake in Illinois. I picked it because there was a big lake there. Good thing we didn't get there the night before in the dark because it was confusing getting a campsite. The off- duty park host told us to save a site because people were driving around trying to get lake sites.

I couldn't figure out where to go because there were tents on all of the good sites, but the notice on the sites said they were expired. I found out later that the rule is that you can save a site with a tent even though you didn't pay for it, which was very strange. There were many loops in this campground and I drove through every one of them looking for a lake front site. Many were flooded and off limits to campers. We finally found a site near the lake, and I put my lawn chair on the site to save it. We had to go get groceries and the park hosts weren't open to pay for the site yet. On our way to the store, we stopped to say hello to the campground deer. There were a lot of them roaming the park, which was really cool to see!

We went to the store and got gas. We even drove through another campground on the way back to see if they had any lake front sites but they didn't. I was tired of driving and ready to start my day on the lake so we headed back to camp.

When we got back, the Ranger had moved our chair and a camper was moving into our site! I was not a happy camper especially after spending nearly an hour finding that site. I am very picky where we camp. It was a good thing that the Ranger pulled up when he did because the campers didn't know what to tell me and plus, it wasn't their fault. It was a bad combination. It was hot. I was hungry and Jack was whining to go swimming. I took it out on the Ranger, poor guy. The rule is that you can save it with a tent but not with a chair, but we didn't know that and why would we have a tent with us when we are in an RV? It was the craziest rule that I had ever heard. I argued so much with him that he felt bad and opened one of the sites for me that was closed due to flooding. We SCORED!

Chapter 18: Illinois

It ended up working out perfectly! We were closer to the lake and Jack got his own little water hole to play in because the site was mostly flooded. I didn't need much, so it didn't matter to me that the grill was under water! It was cute watching him chase little fish in the shallow water. He played in there for over two hours all by himself while I read. His little tail was just wagging away.

The lake was warm and very big. The day that we arrived was very windy so we just swam and hung out with the neighbor kids. They came running over to our site as soon as we arrived. I asked them to give me a couple of minutes to get set up so they went out to the lake to swim and play. They were jumping into the lake from the tree and having a blast! After I ate my lunch, Jack and I headed to the lake. The kids loved swimming with Jack. They were racing with him in the water as if they had a chance! He is a very fast swimmer. They were cute kids, though, and they were having so much fun playing in the lake.

I like playing with kids. As long as they don't touch me we can be friends. These kids were a lot of fun. They would throw the ball in the water, I would jump in after it and then they would jump in and race me to the ball. I let them win a few times just to make them feel good. That is just the kind of dog that I am!

The night was restless because it was very hot and humid therefore I ran my air conditioner all night. When that happens, the constant on and off keeps me awake at night but I was happy to have it!

The next day was beautiful! I inflated the SUP first thing before the wind picked up and we explored the lake. We could see many flooded sites. The neighbor told us that this area had 21" of rain in June, and it had rained for the last two weeks of their stay! Once again our weather gods were with us, because we just missed it!

We stopped a few times to swim and so that Jack could "SUP dive." That means jump off the SUP, swim back, get back on and jump again, then repeat 20 times! It was good entertainment for the anglers. They were wondering if they could SUP, and I offered to let them try. They just laughed!

We got a nice 5 mile leisurely paddle in. When we returned to camp, we invited the neighbor kids and their dog, a hairless Chinese Crested Dog, to get on the SUP. They loved it. It was fun trying to get them all to balance and to get some photos of them. They were laughing and having a great time! They came from a very interesting situation. It sounded like they had a rough childhood, but they were really good kids. I talked to their Grandma for a long time. She was raising them because her daughter was into drugs. I loved hearing her story and how she was giving them the best life that she could. It was very apparent that she loved them a lot and they loved her. It was really a treat to spend the day with them. I gave them a bunch of Jack's Journey USA & KIND snack labels, and they were so excited. They had so much fun swimming with Jack and hanging out with us. The Grandma was telling me how a guy tried to abduct them a few days prior in the campground near the bathroom. It was very scary and just a reminder that you always have to be aware of your surroundings, even when camping.

Chapter 18: Illinois

The people who took our original site came down and were jealous of our site. They had a big group coming and were staying for the July 4th holiday. I guess that is why everyone was saving sites, for the July 4th festivities even though it wasn't for another week and a half. They were also complaining about the strange rules because someone was saving some prime spots next to me on the lake, but they hadn't paid for them yet. They had until the end of the day to pay for them. The people finally did come and dropped off their trailers and boats and then left. I never did see them again!

> **Every campground has different rules so lesson learned. Find out the rules when you arrive. Some of them allow you to pay by putting money in an envelope at the entrance. Some of them make you go to the office. Usually you can save sites with a chair, this campground the rule was it had to be something that you could sleep in. Even though I argued that you can sleep in a chair!**

It was a nice, relaxing stop on our journey. I got a lot of work done while Jack played in his private lake at our site. There were no water hookups, only electric, but that was ok. There were shower rooms and they weren't too bad. Plus, we got to see the deer again on the walk there. There was a running trail that we wanted to explore, but it was too hot so we spent our time hanging out by the lake. We weren't complaining about that.

We walked to the end of our camping area to watch the sunset and met two ladies sipping wine in their camp chairs and enjoying the sunset. They were kayaking all day and came to watch the sunset. It was a never-ending sunset of red skies. If I wouldn't have been talking to them, I probably would have missed it. The best part was a few minutes after the sunset and I probably would have left already. It was so beautiful and another great grand finale to our stay.

The next day, we were off to see our friends in Kansas City. It would be interesting because she has five kids, two dogs and a cat – a little different than what we are used to.

Chapter 19: Missouri

W̶e packed up early from Wayne Fitzgerrell State Park to miss the St Louis morning traffic. It worked because it was an easy drive. We headed to my friends' fitness studios. I am a member of the Todd Durkin Mastermind Group, so I have fitness friends all over the country. I was looking forward to seeing Jill Stoppel-Davis and Mendy Shriver who both had studio's near Kansas City.

It was REALLY hot so, of course, I stopped and let Jack swim on the way on a lake that I spotted while driving. It was interesting because it ended up having a dog park attached to it. The dogs in this area are very lucky! As you know by now, he always gets so excited when I stop and let him swim.

We arrived at Jill's Excel Wellness Studio in Overland Park, Kansas after 1 p.m. It was right on the border of Missouri so it worked out great! We toured her bright studio and met some of her clients. We liked it even more because it was cool in there. Man, it is HOT in these Midwest states! We chatted over lunch and then we were off for Mendy's house.

Mendy lives in Liberty, Missouri, which is north of Kansas City and Jill was south of Kansas City, so it worked out perfect! We were able to visit Mendy's studio as well. It is really fun for us to see the "behind-the-scenes" on how people live.

The Mendy stop was an adventure! She has five kids - three boys of her own and she adopted two girls from Africa. She also has a German Shorthaired Pointer puppy named Sadie who is constantly getting into trouble. After visiting her studio, I found out that her kids had a lot going on that night, so I decided to be the "soccer mom" in the RV! We started the adventure by picking up her dog from the veterinary clinic. She had broken into the tackle box in the garage and got a fishing hook stuck in her lip, so she spent the day at the vet's office. The veterinarian got it out and Sadie was once again a happy dog. While we were there, the vet and half of the staff came to check out Spirit. They were excited about our journey!

After we got Sadie in the RV, we picked up her daughter and took her to the dance studio while the other daughter hung out with us in the RV. It was really fun and interesting to chat with her about Africa. It was a long process for Mendy and her husband to adopt the girls from an orphanage in Africa. I give them a ton of credit because they didn't give up, and now they have saved two beautiful girls and are giving them an amazing life.

We then took her son to his baseball game and her other son to a sleepover at his friend's house. The kids loved riding around in the RV and showing it off to their friends. It is fun and crazy for me to see how people with kids manage their busy schedules. I can't even imagine it, and I give all of the moms out there a BIG kudos! Just managing a household is a full-time job, not to mention all that goes on with kids. Mendy's husband took over the kid duty so she and I could go enjoy dinner.

Wow!! After spending the day at Mendy's house, I wonder what my life would be like if mommy had five kids. I bet I wouldn't be able to do all of the fun things that I do because mommy would have her hands full. I am so happy that I am an only dog!

Mendy and I had dinner at a local restaurant and took Jack because it had a really nice outside deck. Mendy didn't even know that the restaurant named Bell was dog friendly! That is what we are here for – to show people that you can take your dog with you everywhere – even to dinner! Everyone on the deck at the restaurant loved Jack. Since we were in the RV and it was parked near the restaurant, they were looking up JacksJourneyUSA.com on their phones and checking out our blog. It was really fun. Two of Mendy's clients were walking by so I got to meet them. Everyone was so friendly and welcoming.

It was late when we got back to Mendy's house. It was too hot for us to sleep in the RV, so we got to stay in Mendy's beautiful house that her handsome husband built. It was nice to get a shower and sleep in a bed. It was also great to meet Mendy's large and very active family. She definitely has her hands full but she seems to have it under control!

Chapter 20: Kansas

The next morning, we were off to a new state and guess which one? KANSAS! Home of Toto from the Wizard of OZ! This is Jack's 33rd state!

We took the back roads through all of the small Kansas towns to Wamego to visit the Wizard of Oz museum. It was really interesting. They, of course, loved Jack since he is the same breed as Toto - a Cairn Terrier. In fact, they were having a festival in a few months and asked us if we could come because they needed a Toto dog. We told them we wish we could be sorry, we are not hanging out in Kansas for a few months!

Jack got to go into the museum, too, which was a good thing because it was way too hot to stay in the RV. If you take your dog there, you have to carry them or push them in a wheelchair. I opted to carry Jack.

There are a few things that we learned while visiting the museum. Remember that the Wizard of Oz was made in 1939. It wasn't even made in Kansas. It was made in Hollywood. The first thing we learned was that there were 116 "little people" in the movie and they did not use any kids to fill in. I know some of them lived in San Diego because they had special houses built for them.

We also learned that the Tin Man had powder all over his face to make it silver. The powder ended up causing the actor to get emphysema from all of the rehearsals and he ended up in the hospital in an oxygen tent for six weeks and never got to star in the movie. The replacement used a silver makeup instead of the powder and got it in his eye, causing an eye infection. Makeup has come along way since then!

The other cool trivia that we learned is that they used a special material to make the tornado and they pulled it with a car! Crazy stuff! We got to sit in the basket that took Dorothy back to Kansas! One year I dressed up like Dorothy for Halloween and Jack got to go as himself. It would have been funny to have the dress that I wore that year there with me!

It was an interesting stop and broke up the very boring drive through Kansas. Kansas is worse than Texas. There is nothing to look at, and it is very flat. If you plan on driving through that state, I suggest having a good audio book! We knew that we had a BIG carrot on the other end, though. We were heading to COLORADO – our favorite state!

We stayed in a Subway parking lot near a truck stop that night just a little East of Colorado because I was tired and bored from driving. It was ironic because just like the Wizard of OZ, it was a very windy night, and we thought our RV was going to blow over the hillside! It was so windy that Spirit was rocking and the blinds were about to blow off! There was a huge lighting storm too! It was a pretty crazy night!

The next day we were off to Colorado. We will be there for quite a while.

Chapter 21: Colorado

W e moved the RV in the middle of the night to get closer to the building in fear Spirit was going to blow down over the hillside in the wind. We woke up to nobody around except for truck drivers. They were getting coffee at the nearby store, so we joined them! Then we were off! The drive from the Subway parking lot was only 1½ hours to Centennial, Colorado. This will mark our 24th state on our journey.

We arrived at Isabel's house early. It was nice to finally meet her. I had been chatting with her via Facebook and email for almost a year now. Isabel Chamberlin started a program called Paws 4 Fitness in Aurora, Colorado, and we were here to team-teach a class with her.

Staying with Isabel and her husband, Mike, was awesome. They have two dogs, Voodoo and Guinness, and a kitty. Jack got in trouble for chasing the kitty and freaking him out and trapping her under the sofa. He even knocked their lamp over when he climbed behind their sofa and tripped over the cord. He is so embarrassing sometimes. Good thing Isabel is a dog person and she tolerated it. He behaved himself after a day. I think he finally realized he wasn't going to get the kitty to play! Her dogs were great as well.

Yay!! I FINALLY have a kitty to chase! Even though I got in trouble, it was worth it. That kitty was so afraid of me and I loved every minute of it. I would never hurt a kitty, but it sure is fun chasing them!

We all went on a walk near her house. She had a nice trail with a few little water holes where the dogs could cool off. It was fun hanging out with them and seeing her neighborhood. I often wonder what it would be like to live in Colorado, although I would want to live in the mountains somewhere. I am definitely a mountains and trees kind of gal and I love fresh water lakes.

We now have logged more than 8,200 miles on Spirit, so Isabel took us to get an oil change. We had to keep Spirit healthy so we could get home safely! I feel so grateful that Spirit has been so good to us. No mechanical problems whatsoever! Isabel let us do our laundry, take a shower and she fed me all kinds of yummy meals. We slept in the RV under the beautiful Colorado skies next to her driveway.

Guess what else she did? She took us to our first marijuana store! It is legal in Colorado so I had to check it out, plus they allowed Jack to come in. Don't worry, we didn't buy anything, but it was fun to take the tour. It was very clean, well organized and interesting. They had drinks, food, and all kinds of ways to use it. Many people use marijuana for pain, anxiety or a sleep aid as well as many other reasons. They even experiment with it on dogs for anxiety, aggression and other things but you have to be very careful because it is toxic to dogs. It probably won't be long that it is legal everywhere.

She also took us to a drive through mall. It was so cool – like a little mall city complete with a movie theatre and food court. I had never seen anything like it, but then again, I don't shop much. We had dinner there with her husband. He was a really nice guy. We had some good laughs and conversation. I felt so fortunate to have been able to stop here and spend time with them both. They were very hospitable.

The next morning was an exciting day. I got to see my friend, Tamra, who I hadn't seen in over 23 years. We went to X-ray school together in Maryland and after that she got married and started having children. Eventually, I moved to California so we lost touch for many years. We are now friends on Facebook and when I realized that she lived so close we arranged a meeting. It worked out perfectly. She was leaving the next day for a week, so I was lucky that I got to meet up with her. We sat at Starbucks and talked for almost three hours. Tamra and her family move around a lot so I was fortunate that they had moved from Florida to Colorado and lived nearby. It was really fun to catch up on the last 23 years since we graduated. Times were a lot different back then and we had a lot of laughs reminiscing about school. Jack was a good boy and sat patiently and waited. That is one good thing about social media. It helps you to stay connected to people that you otherwise would lose touch with.

Isabel met us there and then we were off to the Boston terrier event that was nearby. We did a little talk there to educate people on a few exercises that they can add to their dog walk, but it was very hot so everyone was more interested in hanging out in the shade. It was fun to meet a few people, and we even recruited a few to our class the following day.

It was HOT there! We went back to Isabel's and had lunch and she decided that we should go to Aurora Reservoir and take the kayak and iSUP out. I was all for that. It had been a few days with little activity so I was ready, and I knew Jack would be, too. I was getting a little cranky with no activity except for driving so a fun paddle sounded perfect. They had weird rules there. People were allowed to swim and have a boat (no gas motors) and dogs were allowed on the boats and other watercraft but not IN the water. Do people think that dogs are dirty or something? Don't they know that ducks are dirtier than dogs? I have a hard time understanding the logic in that. It was a cool lake and a nice lake to paddle on. The front part was full of people but the back part was totally empty except for us!

There was a tree in the middle of the water with a guy tethered to it and relaxing on his SUP. Isabel informed me this was a tree that people jump from. Of course, I had to try it. The guy saw how much fun I was having so he decided to join me. He and I took turns climbing up the tree and jumping out while Isabel took photos. Jack looked at me like I was crazy! Of course, I let him jump in off the SUP, too. I am sure he was not the first dog in that lake. It was a really fun afternoon and just what we needed. Jack and I like to stay active and it felt good to be out on the lake moving around and having a blast!

Chapter 21: Colorado

That night, back at Isabel's house, I was a little worried about my next stop. I was heading to Boulder to meet up with another friend, Shawn Navarro, who lives there. Shawn and I used to work together when I first got the job at University of California at San Diego in 2003. As a matter of fact, we were the only two female X-ray techs back then. She had one day off during the week, so I had a few days in between to be adventurous. There weren't any campgrounds in Boulder, so I was trying to figure out where to go. I decided on the area north of Boulder and decided that I would just drive up in that area and figure it out when I got there.

Most of the state and federal campsites have to be booked on a website called Reserve America or Recreation.gov. When you book sites on those sites, you can't book them after two days prior to your stay. You can look on their website, but it won't tell you what is available as people may have come in and booked sites within that time. I am not sure why they do that and it makes things a little confusing for those of us that wait until the last minute to decide what we are doing. If you do book a site and then cancel, you get charged a cancellation fee. That happened to me when I was going to go to Colorado Springs but changed my mind, so I decided not to try to plan ahead anymore because I was not very good at it and it cost me money. So far everything was working out. I am sure my next stop will work out as well.

Sunday came and it was time to get to work. The best part about class was that I got to see our friends, Shane and Laura Thornwall, from San Diego. They used to be our neighbors. Their dog, Bosco, was Jack's first friend, and he was also one of the very first dogs in our Leash Your Fitness classes. He used to come to the practice classes in 2008 before we even started the business. When I started Leash Your Fitness, I had no idea what I was doing. Before I started our official classes in January of 2009, I would have practice classes at a nearby park to see what worked. I would have my neighbors and friends come and we had fun trying new class formats. Bosco was always up for the task! He moved to Colorado last year with his parents and now he has a little brother. It was so fun to see them and I was so happy that they came to the class. We have been seeing so many of our friends on this trip and I love it!

The class went really well. They were a great bunch of people. There were two pugs there who had endless energy. It was pretty funny. They kept playing and didn't even get tired when they went over the jumps. We have a few pugs in our San Diego classes like these, and they are rare. Most pugs don't have a lot of energy and sadly, it is sometimes because they are overweight. A lot of people think that pugs are couch potatoes. Just like other dogs, they get used to whatever activity that you introduce to them. You just have to be careful because they have a hard time breathing because of their pushed-in muzzles.

> Brachiocephalic dogs like pugs have a shortened noses and undersized breathing passages that hinder their breathing. Bulldogs, Boxers, Pugs, Pekingese, and Boston Terriers fall into this category. It does not mean that they cannot exercise. They just have a harder time breathing and can overheat faster than other dogs. Remember that dogs do not sweat like we do. They pant and release heat through their paws. If they have a hard time breathing in normal situations, then extra attention must be paid to them during exercise.

After class, we went to Starbucks to visit with everyone. It is always a sight to see all of the dogs out on the patio when we go out to breakfast after class. It always draws a lot of attention. It was great to catch up with our friends from San Diego. They love Colorado and they made a really good life there. It was so cool that they got to come to class for old times sake. I got to see a lot of my friends, but it was time to move on to our next adventure – Boulder. I have been all over Colorado camping, but I had never been to Boulder, so I was really excited.

Boulder:

Boulder was only a few hours north of Aurora so it was an easy drive on the freeway. We drove through Boulder – it looked like an active little town. It seemed crowded on this Saturday morning, so I didn't stop plus I was anxious to find a campsite. The 119 road up into the mountains was beautiful. The water was raging coming down the river along the road.

I was so happy. Aurora and Centennial were nice, but they weren't the Colorado that I was used to. I have mountain biked and hiked all over Colorado and love the mountains. Back in 2001, I even did a seven-day bike ride where I rode my bike from Telluride to Moab, Utah and stayed in huts along the way. I love Colorado and was so happy to be back in the mountains. We ended up in a little town called Nederland. Nederland is the base for Estes Park and the ski resort, Eldora. It's a very small town and the day that we drove through, the roads were blocked off for some kind of street fair. We didn't stop. I was on a mission to find a camp spot. It was now summer and a weekend so sites fill up quickly.

I saw that there were a few campgrounds on the 119, so we headed out to see if we could find a site. We passed a National Forest Sign with designated camping areas so I thought it would be fun to check it out. You can camp anywhere in the National Forest for free, so why not?

There were some mountain bikers packing up after a fun day of biking, and I asked one of them if he noticed any open sites back on the dirt road. He said yes, but the road might be a little bumpy for my RV. I thanked him and headed down the road. I was a little concerned about the road, but lucky for us (again!) a guy was leaving in the second site! As we pulled in, we noticed a tent in the corner but Joseph (the guy in the tent) said it was ok to camp there with him, so we did.

I have to admit that I was a little nervous camping in the same site with a stranger, and I almost left twice. He probably thought I was crazy because I kept pulling out and then backing back into the site. But I felt like God led me there for a reason, so I would just chance it. He hadn't led me astray yet! It ended up working out perfectly. Joseph was just trying to get back on his feet, so he was living in his tent for a while and working in Nederland. He turned out to be a really nice guy.

It was a beautiful area and once again, I was feeling so grateful! It was getting late and the clouds were rolling in and it started thundering, but we went for a little hike on the West Magnolia Trails anyhow. It was beyond what we could have ever imagined. There were snow-covered mountains in the distance, a little pond and trails everywhere! We were in heaven! When we got back to camp, Joseph was laughing at us because we were barely parked and out hiking. He said he could tell that we were in our element, and he was right! Have I said that I LOVE Colorado?

We woke up on Monday to a beautiful day! We were so excited to go explore the trails. We met our other neighbors from Site 1 on the way to the trailhead. There were three of them in that site, and they all lived in their tents. They were telling me they walk a mile to a spring to get water when they run out. They were really nice people with crazy life stories of how they got to live in tents. One guy was from Texas and he was telling me how he lived in a cave in Texas all winter and then took a bus to Colorado for the summer. We sure have met a lot of interesting people on this trip. Everyone has a story, and I love hearing them and learning about people. It really is one of the highlights of travel. I don't judge. I think most people will treat you how you treat them - with respect and trust. We all have to watch out for each other!

The hike was awesome. For once, I did a smart thing and took a photo of the trail map at the kiosk before we left. It helped because I hadn't stopped in Nederland and I didn't have any trail maps. I am glad that I did that because there were trails everywhere, and we got to hike most of them. We even hiked trails that weren't on the map. I accidentally turned my GPS off when I was on one of them and then couldn't get it back on because we were so far in the trees. I wasn't sure where the trail that we were on was going since it wasn't on the map. The only person I saw the entire day was a mountain biker, and he rode past while I was taking a photo from a rock. I didn't even get to talk to him and find out where we were, so I decided to eventually turn around and head back the way we came. I love it when we are the only ones on the trails. I love the solitude. I love listening to nature. I just love being with Jack and watching how much fun he has.

The 726 trail had a great overlook and was a trail where Jack could cool off in the little stream! The 355 was the road that connected all of the trails and the one with the little pond on it where Jack could swim. The 925 was the trail that overlooked Nederland and had the horse corral and lots of poop for Jack to roll in! I was not happy about that part. I think he did it on purpose so I would take him back to the pond to wash off, and he could swim again. This dog has me figured out!

After hiking 11 miles, we were done for the day. We loved camping in this national park. Our neighbors came over to see how we liked the trails. We told them about trails that they didn't even know about even though they had been here for over a week. It was interesting talking to them. They said that this area would be full of people in a few days because of the 4th of July holiday. They also said that there are a band of transients that come though by the thousands. This particular group is on the East Coast right now, but they travel to each National Forest and spend the maximum of two weeks. Then they move on. I am glad that they weren't here taking up all of the sites, because we enjoyed our stay. It is amazing how many people live in tents, RVs and campers around the country. I just may have to try it one day!

This find was exactly why I don't like booking campsites ahead of time. I never know what kind of detour I can find that will be more fun and best of all - FREE! It is what seasoned campers call, Boondocking. Camping off of the grid for free. Most National Forests and Bureau of Land Management (BLM) land allow free camping.

The next morning, we got up early to get to Boulder. I wanted to get a little work done at Starbucks before we met Shawn, since obviously we didn't have WiFi in the National Forest. We gave Joseph a ride to work in Nederland, wished him the best and gave him a little goody bag to remember us by. I really do hope he figures things out so he can move out of the tent before winter!

It was so fun to see Shawn. I haven't seen her since she worked with me nearly eight years ago! We decided to hike up Chautauqua Mountain in Boulder to the Flatirons. The hike is a very popular hike and there were a lot of people there that day. I was very lucky to find a spot to park Spirit. It was free parking so I was able to leave her there all day while we hiked, and then went and had lunch in Boulder.

It was a little warm, so I would suggest leaving early if you are going to do this hike with your dog. We stopped a lot in the shade so we could chat and Jack could cool off. It was a really beautiful and rocky hike. There were a few trails to choose from. We hiked up between the 1st and 2nd Flatirons. There were outstanding views, and it was really fun to catch up with Shawn. This journey is like a reunion with so many old friends and family.

After the hike, we met Shawn's husband for lunch in Boulder at the Pearl Street Mall. The entire mall is outside but we found out that it is not dog friendly. I couldn't believe it. We were told it is because there are so many transients in the area and most of them have dogs. The city doesn't want them hanging out in the mall. I was bummed because it was a really cool mall, and I wanted to walk through it and check it out. I went into Illegal Pete's on the corner and asked the manager if we could eat on his patio. He was a really nice guy and said that we could eat on their patio as long as Jack didn't bite anyone. It was a deal! Jack was tired from the hike and the heat so he just laid by my feet while we enjoyed lunch. They had really good food, and it was fun to sit and people watch and chat with Shawn and her husband.

We spent the night at Shawn's house in Broomfield. Shawn has two sweet little girls and a cute Boxer puppy. We took everyone for a walk when we got home and saw a beautiful rainbow. Once again, it was fun to walk through the neighborhood. They are all so different and it is fun to see where people live. It started to rain just as we got back to the house.

I was happy to get a shower at Shawn's house since I hadn't had one in a few days. When camping in the National Forest we only had the water that was in our tank in the RV. I hadn't filled it up prior to going, and I used it sparingly. Needless to say, a hot shower felt good! Jack found a comfortable chair that he crashed out in. He wasn't used to being around two little girls who wanted to pet him, plus a puppy who really wanted to play with him. It was a little stressful for him, but he handled it well.

I set my alarm for 6 a.m. the next morning so I could see Shawn before she left for work. It was a short visit but I was very happy to see her and appreciated her allowing us to stay at her house. She made me some really strong coffee press coffee and then left for work. The coffee kicked in and I got a ton of work done on my computer. I always take advantage of the internet when it is available. I also got my clothes washed. Camping is a dirty sport!

We really loved Boulder. I wish we could have stayed longer and explored the area a little bit, but we had to leave because it was 4th of July weekend and once again, we didn't know where we were staying. Campsites would fill up for sure, so once again, we were on another adventure!

Twin Lakes:

We stopped a few times after leaving Boulder. We usually do not like highways, but the I-70 through Colorado is beautiful! I rewarded Jack again since he is such a good travel partner by stopping to let him swim in Georgetown Lake. It was really cold, but he didn't care. The snow-capped mountains behind the lake were breath taking. I love

Colorado! (Have I emphasized that enough?)

I had to cover him up when he got out because he was shaking. He laid in his car seat, and I turned on the heater for him. Yes, he is a spoiled dog, but he is such a good boy so he deserves it! We headed down I-91 to Leadville. We stopped at a lake there, too, but Jack didn't swim. I just enjoyed the scenery and talked to the other people there. They were very interested in our journey. It was fun telling them where we have been and where we are going. Jack kept busy chasing varmints. That is what Cairn terriers were bred to do!

We didn't really know where we were going, so we stopped in Leadville. It sits at 10,000 feet elevation. It is known for the Leadville Trail 100 - a 100-mile trail race that takes part once a year and brings people from all over the world to compete. I went into a few of the shops and enjoyed the town.

We were going to stay at the campground there for one night because we needed to fill our water tank and to dump our grey and black water tanks. In addition, I wasn't sure where else to stay. We stopped in the ranger station and the ranger told us about the dump station across the road for only $5! That was the deal of a lifetime. She also told us about a few campgrounds south of there. We met a couple at the dump station that live in and work out of their RV. The gal just happened to be from San Diego. She was intrigued by our RV and wanted to hear about our journey. She said that they were on their way to Crested Butte if we wanted to join them, but I really didn't feel like driving that far. We exchanged numbers just in case I changed my mind, they were super nice. I find people who live in their RVs full time to be very intriguing. I love chatting with them about all of the places that they have been so you will meet this couple again later!

We headed to Twin Lakes because we like to go where there is water. First, we stopped at a campground that was basically a parking lot except it was on the water. There was nobody camped in it. The park host said that we had our pick of sites, but I was not impressed. So we moved on to the next one. The second campground had only a few sites that were available, and I didn't like them, so we drove up the road to the third campground. This one was not near the lake or any hiking so that was not going to work for me, either. If you haven't noticed, I am very picky where I camp. I like to park the RV and be able to walk everywhere. The final campground was Lakeview, and it was almost perfect!

The park host, Bill, was really nice. There were no hookups or a dump station, but it was only $19 a night. Since we were going to be staying here for four nights, Bill said he would let us use his hose to fill up my water tank again so I could take a shower if I wanted to.

I still wasn't sold that there would be enough for us to do for four days plus we weren't right on the lake. I am getting spoiled. We usually only stay two nights at each site, but because of the holiday weekend we decided to stay four. I took a walk around the campground to check it out. Our nice neighbors told us about the Colorado Trail, Mount Elbert and the trail to the lake, all within walking distance. Ok, I was sold!

There was plenty to do and all of the campers that we met on our walk were really helpful and nice like most campers are. We walked down to the lake, and Jack swam for a few minutes. The neighbors acted like it was a really far walk. I think it was less than a mile, and we even got to walk under the road through a tunnel. I have learned not to take what people say to heart. Back in the day when I used to mountain bike, people would always tell us how hard certain trails were and they we would do them and they were easy for us. It is all relative, so I just listen and figure it out for myself.

I went back to the RV and researched Mount Elbert. It turns out that it is the tallest peak in Colorado at 14,433 feet high, ranking as the second highest in the lower 48 states. I wasn't sure if either Jack or I were up for the challenge, but I was certainly going to try it! The highest we had ever hiked was over 12,000 feet in Idaho on a road trip that we had done there a few years prior. During that hike, my legs felt like they weighed a ton, kind of like I was walking on the moon! An 80-year-old man passed me, which gave me the incentive to press on. Of course, he lived there and had done it a few times. Still, he was 80! I was so inspired by him, I got my photo taken with him at the top of the mountain. I love it when older people are still out doing fun things and living their life.

When I spoke to our neighbors about their hike to Mount Elbert, I found out only four of the 12 who started made it to the top. It took them a long time to get there, and they only stayed at the top for a short time before the clouds moved in and it was time to head back down before the rain. I was intrigued and felt that a few days in the area and on the trail would help with getting acclimated to the altitude.

We woke up the next morning and took off on the Colorado Trail. Wow!! What a great trail right from our camp! The

Chapter 21: Colorado

Colorado trail runs from Denver to Durango so obviously, we didn't do the entire thing. We hiked five miles and then turned around and came back on the trail and then returned to camp on the 4-wheel drive road. The elevation gain was from 9,000 feet at camp to 10,000 feet where we turned around. So far, Jack was doing fine in the elevation.

The section of the trail that we hiked had beautiful Aspen trees and some fallen timber. We even found a few beaver ponds where Jack got to do his favorite thing - SWIM! I was glad that we didn't turn around when it started to cloud up and thunder because the trail was so beautiful! It just kept going and going and going. It seemed each bend was something new to see. There was a giant meadow, and I was hoping to see some wildlife in it, but no such luck. It never did rain and the sun eventually came back out. The weather is very unpredictable in Colorado, so you have to be prepared for anything.

We came back on the 125B 4-wheel drive road because I wanted to check it out for the day that we hike Mount Elbert. There was no way that I could drive the RV up this road. It was going to be all up hill to the trailhead, so I decided that we were going to hitch a ride to cut off two miles. No point wasting our energy on a road.

After our hike, our neighbors had us over for dinner. They were from a church near Liberty, MO where our friend Mendy lives and where we just were a few weeks ago! Once again I am amazed that it is such a small world!

I woke up on the next day to rain! I was disappointed, but it stopped around 9 a.m. We packed up and drove the RV to

Twin Lakes at the bottom of the hill to the first campground that we had stopped at to SUP. This was the campground that was a parking lot. Now, it was full of campers and tents were scattered all over the lakeside. It was actually really cool, and the tent sites had awesome views of the lake. I decided it was probably a good idea to give Jack's legs a break before we did our big hike the next day, so we spent the day on the lake.

There were actually two lakes, which is why it was called Twin Lakes. We SUP'd both of them! Nine miles total and the lakes were like glass, making for an easy, enjoyable paddle. Of course, Jack got to go in and swim, too! We met a family who were in inflatable kayaks. It was the Grandma, daughter and two kids. We had a nice chat session out in the middle of

the lake. I inspired the Grandma to start traveling in an RV. She said she had always wanted to do it, but didn't know if it would be safe for a woman to travel alone. I assured her that it was and gave her some resources to check out. I hope that she really does it!

We also met a couple from Denver who previously lived in Antarctica. They said it would get 103 degrees below zero there. I can't even imagine that. I could have sat and talked to them all day. They were so interesting. It is not every day that you meet people that lived in Antarctica! I absolutely LOVE meeting new people. You learn so much and people are so fascinating. The world is such a large place and it is fun meeting people that have lived all over.

It started clouding up and getting really windy. It even started thundering at the end of our paddle, so I started paddling a little harder to get back to where we started. The weather in Colorado is so tricky. I didn't really want to be on the water if it stormed, especially thunder and lightening. It ended up blowing past and then getting warm again while I was enjoying my much-deserved lunch in the RV.

We got back to camp and took the site that our neighbors had. It was the best site in the entire camp. It was at the end of the road, on the edge and overlooking the lake. I felt so blessed to be there! It was like we were at the top of the world! It even had a heart-shaped stone formation around it. I rolled my legs out on my foam roller and stretched on our picnic table while enjoying the beautiful view! Once again, we totally scored with ending up at this campground with all of the fun things to do and the beautiful views. It went from "almost" perfect to PERFECT!

I got to bed early for our big hike tomorrow. I was a little nervous about it. I didn't really have the right equipment with me, but I made do. I had everything ready to go so we could wake up at 4:45 a.m. and be at the road early to hitch a ride the two miles on the bumpy road to the trailhead.

Mount Elbert:

For a brief moment when the alarm went off at 4:45 a.m., I thought about turning it off. I am so happy that I didn't. I packed up, fed Jack and ate my banana with almond butter. Of course, I also had my coffee. Coffee is a must before 5 a.m.! I walked in the dark to the road and only stood there for a few minutes until a car approached. I hitched a ride from a family of four. It was great to see that their little kids were going to do this hike. I love to see kids out enjoying nature. I don't really think that they wanted to give me a ride, but they did and I was grateful. I wasn't sure what this hike was going to entail, and I didn't want to waste energy walking two miles up a dirt road to get to it. I knew that someone would stop since everyone hiking from this side of the mountain has to either drive or walk up the road.

The hike up was not as hard as the time we hiked to 12,000 feet in Idaho. I am not sure why – maybe it was because it was a shorter hike. It was five miles up from the trailhead. Straight up!

The Mount Elbert trail started in the Aspen trees at 10,440 feet elevation. There was a dirt parking area at the trailhead and at 6 a.m., already had a few cars there. There were also places along the road to camp. It was National Forest area so you could camp anywhere for free. It was too bad the road couldn't accommodate Spirit. It would have been really cool to camp out there.

It didn't take long before we were above tree line, and it got windy. I wished I had brought my buff to protect my ears, but I used my extra shirt instead. I tied it around my head. Sexy, I know! It wasn't windy for long. It was a really beautiful and sunny day. We lucked out! If we had done this yesterday we would have been starting in the rain, which would not have been fun! I probably would have turned the alarm off then!

I never felt like the hike was that hard, but it may have been because we have been hiking a lot over the past seven weeks, and we have been in Colorado at altitude for a week now. We passed a few people. One guy had his 7-year-old son hiking with him. He was so cute. He made sure to tell me how old he was! At one point, we had to hike around a patch of snow. We lost the trail here, but quickly figured it out. I could see something on the top of a ridge, and it turned out to be people! That was where we were going!

We got to the top of the highest peak in Colorado and the second highest in the country in three hours. The elevation gain was around 3,000 feet in five miles, so it was all ascents. I stopped a lot to take photos and enjoyed the views. It was 4th of July, so it was very festive at the top! A few people had large flags and since there was not an official sign at the top with the elevation on it, people made cardboard ones. We all took turns getting our photo taken with it. There were people of all ages at the top and a lot of dogs. One guy was there on his mountain bike! He was having a blast. He drank a beer at the top. I bet the ride down was better than the push up! We stayed at the top for two hours talking to people and enjoying the view! The clouds didn't move in and we enjoyed the beautiful Colorado day and experience!

Jack did amazing on the hike. He was running around all over the place chasing the varmints. We stopped on the way down and played in the snow. It was cool that we could see where we SUPed yesterday! We had a perfect view of Twin Lakes.

It really heated up, so we stopped at the beaver ponds on the way back, so Jack could go swimming to cool off. He had endless energy, and we were both really enjoying the day. Most of the cars that were there when we started were gone. I had seen the family that gave me a ride up the road at the top. They didn't talk to me, but I was happy to see that they made it. They didn't stay at the top as long as I did, so they beat me down and were gone. They were probably worried that I was going to ask them for a ride back too. I was happy to walk the road back down. If I had known we were going to do so well on the hike, I would have walked it up!

What a 4th of July to remember! I was so proud of Jack. I kept giving him big hugs and telling him how much I love him. Of course, I do that every day, so it was nothing new! After 13 miles of hiking, playing in the snow, chasing squirrels and swimming, he was ready for a nap. I, on the other hand, felt like I was on an adrenaline high. I stopped and told the neighbors all about our day whether they wanted to hear about it or not. They were excited for us too. I was so excited that the weather was so good and that we both did so well on the hike.

I sat and watched the sunset that night and felt so grateful for another glorious day and that we were both safe and healthy enough to be able to do a hike like the one that we just did. I really couldn't have asked for a more perfect four days. Twin Lakes ended up being a really fun stop! Sometimes the best things in life are totally unplanned!

Crested Butte:

I hated to leave the campsite at Twin Lakes. Originally, I didn't think we would want to stay there, and it ended up being a GREAT stop. Our campsite was so perfect overlooking the lake. Our travel spirits treated us right again. I won't doubt them anymore!

I stopped on my way out and gave Bill and his wife, the campground hosts some KIND bars and thanked them for being so KIND to us. That is what I did everywhere I went on the trip. KIND Snacks was one of our sponsors. It was another fluke coincidence getting them on board. I had emailed them to tell them about my trip and ask if they wanted to sponsor me and while waiting for a response, an ironic connection happened. A week later, I was asking one of the girls who had just started coming to our classes how her job was going. She said that she didn't like it and had just applied to work for KIND Snacks! Can you believe that? So I asked her for the contact info. I emailed him and they were all for getting the KIND name out there. I loved having the bars with me to hand out to KIND people along my journey!

The drive down the 24 was beautiful with lots of raging water. I stopped a few times to take photos. I stopped in Buena Vista because I needed to use the WiFi somewhere. Unfortunately, it was so crowded! The 4th of July holiday weekend plus a car show and farmer's market was too much for me, especially when I was used to camping in quiet solitude. Lucky for us, we just happened to park next to a hotel with free WiFi. How lucky is that? I got some work done in the RV while Jack slept.

We got on the 50 and had to go over Monarch Pass, it was raining and the road was super steep! We passed right over the Continental Divide. We have been at the 45th parallel and now the Continental Divide. Those are pretty cool landmarks to see. My dad used to say if you peed on the Continental Divide, half would go to the Atlantic Ocean and half would go to the Pacific Ocean. He was always saying crazy stuff like that.

If you have never been to Crested Butte, you are missing out. It is such a cute little town. It was rainy when we arrived around 4 p.m., so we just walked around the town and checked things out. Most of the stores were very expensive, but it was fun looking around.

We were meeting the couple that we met at the dump station in Leadville last week. Drea and Seth have been staying in the National Forest in Gunnison National Forest ever since we saw them. They invited us to join them for a few days. I met them at a bar to watch the World Cup Soccer game. It was really exciting because the US women WON. I am not really into soccer, but it was electric in the restaurant and standing room only. Jack was happy to stay in the RV and sleep some more. He was catching up from our last four busy days of hiking and swimming.

Chapter 21: Colorado

After the game, we headed out to the camping area. It was on a dirt road called Washington Gulch. We had to take it a few miles over some bumps until we got to the place where Drea and Seth were camping. Oh my God! It was BEAUTIFUL! It was exactly like I remembered from the last time I was in Crested Butte in 2001. My friend, James, and I mountain biked all over Colorado including this area. It was full of wild flowers then, and it is again now. We parked right in the middle of them on a little dirt road.

Jack was in doggy heaven. He jumped out of the RV and immediately started chasing all of the critters. There were campers spread out all over and everyone had dogs. It was like a giant dog park!

The next day was a little chilly and cloudy. For some reason, I didn't sleep well at all so it was a slow morning. Jack couldn't wait to go out and run around the flowers. He even stopped and smelled a few of them. He was just so busy chasing all of the critters and smelling all of the smells. It sure does make me smile to see him having so much fun. He is going to be so depressed when we go home. He has had the time of his life on this journey. There has been so much freedom!

Our other neighbors, Kim and Ken own The Nordic Inn in Crested Butte. They have a house there, too, but they love it out here so much that they just spend a lot of time in their trailer here. I can't say that I blame them! Their little Boston terriers go everywhere with them, even mountain biking and skiing. Ken showed me a video of them in the snow. They were really wild with a ton of energy. They came running into our RV and jumped into Jack's car seat. It was really funny.

I had never seen such active Boston Terriers. I think dogs acclimate to whatever they are used to. If you start exercising them early and they get used to it, they expect it and crave it just like people do. I know Jack does!

Kim dropped us off at the Snodgrass trailhead on her way to work because she was afraid that I wouldn't see the trailhead if I walked down the road. It was a super fun hike and not too difficult. Jack and I were both tired today so this hike was perfect. It was three miles each way, but we took a few side trails along the way to explore because that is what we like to do.

It was a very popular mountain biking trail and there were a lot of them on the trail. I remember riding this exact trail 14 years ago! You could start near the town from a super fun trail. A few of the bikers even had their dogs running

alongside them. Dogs are super active around here! We love that!

The hike took forever because I was taking a ton of photos of the beautiful views with the flowers and the mountains. It was breathtaking here. I almost didn't come to Crested Butte because it was out of the way. You have to drive 30 miles up a road to get to it and then return on that road to get back on course, but I am so happy that I decided to come here for a few days. It is definitely worth it, and you can't beat free camping in a flower field overlooking the mountains!

We walked home from the trail and saw some horses that were camped near us. They had a dog running with them, too! It was so refreshing to see dogs just running free and not on a leash. There are no leash laws in the national forest so, for once, we are not breaking the law. Jack is almost always off leash when it is safe for him to be. He listens really well, and he actually walks better without the leash. We are lucky that after 10 years, we have never had a ticket. It probably helps that he is very well behaved and so cute! I know many people are very against this practice but it works for us.

Since Jack accidentally (on purpose) rolled in horse poop AGAIN, I walked him down to the stream near our camp and let him go in the stream to get rinsed off. It wasn't very deep, but it did the trick.

We ended our nine-mile hike just in time for the rain to start. I took a hot shower in the RV and Jack took a nap! It was nice hanging out in the RV listening to the rain. It didn't last long and then the sun came back out. Break time is over!

Just as the rain stopped, we got a new neighbor. Chris just got this new retro camper. It was awesome. It looked old, but it was really brand new. He lived in it full time, too. We met a lot of full-time campers. He had a job that he can do from anywhere, so he said he was spending so much time driving every weekend from LA to go and camp that he thought, "What the heck - why not do it full time?" He just started not too long ago and loved it. There seemed to be a network of full time campers. Chris had met Drea and Seth somewhere else, and the other couple that was camping here was part of the network too. It really would be a fun way to live if you had a job that was online. They were all pretty young and working full-time from their campers!

That night I had a nice relaxing night to just hang out and read and then, I finally got a good night sleep. I'm not sure if it was the altitude, but I hadn't slept well since arriving in Colorado. It was nice to finally sleep! Jack was sleeping in his car seat in the front so he could look out the window at the critters. In the morning, he couldn't get out of the RV fast enough! He ran down to the new campers who came in last night via motorcycles. I went down to say hi and found out one of the guys was a radiologist and the other a male nurse. They were tired of the medical field, so they were taking some time off to travel around the country and camp. I met people from every profession, every age and every state but they all had one thing in common, they were very adventurous people and loved traveling!

Grand Mesa:

I have to say that it was very sad leaving Crested Butte. I feel like I say that every time that I leave a campsite because

Chapter 21: Colorado

I have been staying in some amazing places! We didn't stay very long in Crested Butte, and it would have been fun to stay a few extra days and explore. We had a fun visit, and it reminded me of how much I love it there. I will go back again someday. I stopped on the way out to dump our RV and get more water. There was a $10 Dump station in town that came in handy. Then we were off and heading to Grand Mesa.

I stopped at Gunnison Reservoir to let Jack get out and swim. There was no way I was going to be able to pass that huge lake without him noticing it. The clouds were moving in very quickly so we ran to the lake. He barely got out of the water and we returned to the RV when a HUGE storm hit! It was pouring! The storms in Colorado don't mess around! I sat in the parking lot for a few minutes because I really didn't want to drive in the storm. It was coming down so hard.

Kim told me to take the 92 up through the mountains to Grand Mesa, but it was pouring down rain when we passed the 92, and it did not look like a road that I wanted to be on in the storm so we stayed on the 50. We lucked out and the storm subsided long enough for us to visit Black Mountain National Park. I am glad that I took the side road up and checked it out. It was worth driving out of the way to see. There was a $15 entrance fee which I did not mind paying. It was definitely worth it. There were not many trails to hike, but the lookouts were awesome! Not many people were out exploring, so we had a few of the lookouts all to ourselves. I got some beautiful photos. I have been to the Grand Canyon, but this was completely different.

There was a river at the bottom and the canyons were very steep on either side.

We got a photo of the highest cliff in Colorado. It is 2300 feet high. The sign said that if the Empire State Building stood on the canyon floor, it would only reach halfway to the top of the cliff! It is crazy to think about it like that.

Once again, our weather Gods were with us because as soon as we left the park, it started raining again and rained the rest of our drive! We stopped at the forest station at the bottom of the road before driving up the Grand Mesa to find out about camping. The lady there told me that there was no dispersed camping on the lakes and that all sites with electric hookups had to be reserved. Both of those statements were false, but at least I got a map so it was worth the stop. I drove straight to Island Lake Campground in the Grand Mesa National Park. We got a site with electric on it so I could charge my laptop and use heat. There were plenty of sites available, so I took the one that was the most level.

It stopped raining again so I took Jack down to the lake to check it out. It was a really pretty lake, but the mosquitos were horrible. It looked like there was a trail that went along the lake that we could check out in the morning. It started raining again and was supposed to rain the next couple of days, so I wasn't sure what all we were going to be able to do. Grand Mesa is the largest mesa in the world and there are over 300 lakes. It would be a shame not to at least SUP on one of them!

It was cold and gloomy in the morning. We decided we better get going before it started to rain, so we headed down the lake trail. I was bummed that I did not wear my running gear because it was a perfect running trail. It was 1.7 miles to RT 65. Across the street was another lake and the Visitor

Center. It just happened to be my 47th birthday and we had no cell or Internet reception at the campground, so I went over to the Visitor Center to see if they did. It was a good thing that the Visitor Center had free WiFi because I had a bunch of Happy Birthday messages via text, voice mail and Facebook! It would have been rude not to reply to them! It made me feel really good that people didn't forget about me while we were away. But how could they? I had been posting photos daily on our Leash Your Fitness Facebook and Instagram pages and posting blog posts at every stop on JacksJourneyUSA.com. Everyone was following our journey and enjoying it with us!

We had to get back and move Spirit from our campsite before the checkout time, so we decided to move to Little Bear Campground. It was the next campground over, and we got a site right on the lake! We took off again for another hike because it wasn't raining yet! We found so many cool trails and lakes everywhere. Ward Lake was another cool lake with campsites on it.

The water was pretty cold. Even Jack wasn't sure if he wanted to go in, but of course he did! We also saw deer and a bunch of marmots. They were screaming to each other. I kept trying to get close to get a photo of them. They were very interested in us, but they would hide as soon as I would get close. They were really cute and you only see them at elevation so it was a treat to see some.

It was fun exploring. It seemed that one trail would run into another trail that would run into another trail, and there were lakes on all of them!

We went back to the visitor center and the ranger told us we should just park in dispersed camping for free. Then he told us a few places to go. We went and moved Spirit. Andy, the camp host, was a great guy. He didn't even know that we had left him a check, so he gave us back our check and didn't care that we left. As a matter of fact, he agreed with us. We ended up taking the 121 and there were houses, ATV rentals and even a little resort on that road. We camped right on Eggleston Lake, in the parking lot next to an older couple with their grandchild. They were enjoying the day fishing. They warned me about a baby brown bear that they had seen yesterday in the area. I was originally going to hike from here the next day but on second thought, I will hike from the other side even though, I am sure there are brown bears over there as well!

It was a beautiful lake. We parked just in time before steady rain began. It was thundering and lightening for a while. It was great sleeping weather, and we both slept really well. Once again, another great day, and I couldn't have asked for a better birthday!

The next morning, we woke to a beautiful sunrise over the mountain. The fog on the lake was amazing and mesmerizing to watch. It was only 45 degrees outside but felt much warmer and looked like it was going to be a much nicer day! I sat and stared at the lake and thought about this journey that we have been on. I don't think it was coincidence that everything kept happening so perfectly for us. I have never been very religious, but this trip has been very spiritual for me. At one point, I had to stop worrying about things and just let things happen. Incredibly, they always did.

Someone was watching out for us, and I really appreciated it. We have met so many interesting people, we have done so many amazing things, Spirit has been running great and the weather has cooperated 90 percent of the time. I feel so blessed to be another year older, and I feel much wiser. I don't feel the need to control everything. Instead, sometimes I just have to stop and listen to what I am told to do and trust that the outcome is going to work out.

We left the lake and stopped at the visitor center to check in and reply to more birthday messages. It wasn't open yet so I just sat outside on their deck. It was kind of nice not having Internet on my birthday. I probably would have been checking my phone all day instead of enjoying the trails, lakes and scenery like I did. Sometimes, it is nice to unplug. I am starting to enjoy it more and more! But I did appreciate all of the kind messages that I received!

It is 9 a.m. and we are at the trailhead ready for our last epic hike. There are two options on the Crag Crest Trail. You can just do the lower trail, which is four miles at 10,000 feet or do the entire loop, which is 10.5 miles to over 11,000 feet. Of course, we did the entire loop.

We hiked through Aspen trees, rockslides, pine trees and flowers. It was a great hike. The scenery kept changing and there was always something new to see. From the top, we could see over 15 lakes. We hiked the rim and there were a lot of pretty flowers to see and views on both sides. We even got to play in the snow at the top and, of course, Jack got to go swimming toward the bottom. There was one section with a bunch of blown over trees. We walked through them, which was cool because an hour earlier we looked down from the top and saw them. It is always interesting to look and see where you have been and what you have accomplished. This goes for hikes as well as with life! So often I think that we trudge through just looking down and not enjoying the journey.

It was a beautiful day. There was no rain until the very end when it started sprinkling. You have to get an early start in the mountains because it rains most afternoons. We met a few people on the trail and sat and chatted with them. It was fun to see people of all ages out on the trail. Some older folks were lost, and I had to help them figure out which way to go which is ironic because I am usually the one lost!

It was a very emotional day for me. It was our last big day of our journey. I spent the day thinking back at each stop that we had made on this trip and thought of all of the wonderful people that we met. I felt so blessed – not only to be able to take the time to make this trip, but to have memories that will last my lifetime. Some of them were life changing. I met a lot of people who were traveling and a lot of people who said, "I can't wait to do that when I retire" when they heard what I was doing.

I wonder, why wait? Why can't you do the things that you want to do before you retire. I think so often people say, "I will do that when this happens." Well, I hate to tell them but THIS may never happen. I am happy that my dad gave me his adventurous spirit. My dad retired when he was 53 years old. He said he didn't need to make any more money. It was time to enjoy life and he did. He golfed, traveled, floated down the river in a canoe and even bungee jumped from a hot air balloon when he was in his 70s! I hope I am still doing adventurous activities when I am in my 80's!

The hike took five hours, and I was very hungry when we got done. I sat in the RV in the parking lot and ate my lunch.

Chapter 21: Colorado

I didn't want to leave because I knew it meant the trip was rapidly coming to an end. Plus, I didn't know where we were going to stay that night. I headed back to the visitor center to ask Paul, the friendly ranger who was now like a friend, where I should stay. He suggested a few roads where I could just pull over and stay alongside the road for the night. So we headed back down the 65 on our way out of Grand Mesa. A few of the roads that he suggested were very bumpy, and I didn't feel like driving on them. I took one road and I was happy that my sister wasn't with me because there was no guardrail, and it was straight down to the lake below! Roads like that freak her out. I ended up just pulling into another parking lot by Jumbo Lake, and camping there for the night.

Of course, it started raining as soon as I parked! I finally had cell service so I made all of my phone calls, returned a ton of emails and did other things that required internet service since I hadn't really had any for the last couple of days. This was my last night in Colorado and I was very sad. As you know by now, I love Colorado. I love the people, the lifestyle, and the mountains and now, I love the free camping! I would seriously consider moving here, but I am not a fan of cold weather or snow. The people here say that it is different from where I grew up on the East Coast. It can be snowing one day and 70 the next. I could probably get used to that, so who knows? Maybe I will move here one day! I am more of a mountains gal than a beach gal, but you can't beat the weather in San Diego plus I have a pretty fun life there.

 *I would be okay with mommy's decision to move to Colorado. I would like the fresh water lakes to swim in instead of the yucky salt water. I would also like hiking in the mountains every day. If you haven't noticed, I like to stay active!*

Of course, I woke up early and got on the road. It wasn't like there was anything to do in the parking lot on Jumbo Lake. I didn't see any hikes or anything around there. Plus, I wasn't sure if there would be traffic around Grand Junction.

The drive from Grand Mesa down the 65 was really pretty. I am glad I did it during sunrise through the mountains. That is why I do not like driving at night. You miss so much of the scenery! Out of curiosity and because I needed gas, I drove through the entire town of Grand Junction. It looked like an older town with new developments being built on the outskirts. It was surrounded by mountains and was really pretty.

I said it before, but the drive on the 70 in Colorado is awesome. It continued into Utah. I kept stopping and taking photos. I love all of the colored rocks in Utah. It sure is a change of scenery for us. It made my sadness a little better having beautiful scenery all around us.

Chapter 22: Utah

Once again, I wasn't sure where to go for our last night on the trip, but I knew I had to go somewhere near water as it was a warm day! I settled for Sand Hollow Reservoir near Hurricane, and we got to camp on the red sand. It was definitely an adventure. I almost got stuck driving in but I was proud of myself for making it.

As soon as we parked the RV, I started inflating the iSUP. Jack was going crazy! He kept running back and forth from the RV to the lake while I was inflating the SUP. He won't go in the water until I say it is okay, and it was killing him. He couldn't wait to swim in that huge lake.

It was a big lake, and the water was warm! We were both so happy that we paddled to the other side of the lake. The red rock formations surrounding the lake were really cool. We docked the SUP and went climbing up the rocks. As we got to the top, I noticed a big crowd on the other side. People were jumping off of the rocks into the water! I was super disappointed because I really wanted to do it, but I knew if I left Jack at the top of the rocks and jumped in, he would freak out. I didn't want him running down the rocks looking for me and get hurt. So I decided not to.

It was the only time on my entire trip that I wished I would have had someone else with me. It was fun watching everyone have a good time. We paddled all around looking at all of the red rocks. If you have never been in Utah, it is a treat. The rock formations are unlike anywhere else. They are so beautiful to look at and climb on. Your feet just stick to them! Plus, we hadn't been on our SUP for a while so it felt good to be paddling and in warm water.

The paddle back was really a good workout. We had a strong head wind. There were whitecaps on the lake. It took us a while to get back, which was okay. It was a nice day with no chance of rain for a change!

It was amazing how many people arrived while we were gone. There were campers set up on either side of us, and a bunch of young boys next to us were running their generator. It was really annoying listening to a generator when we were trying to relax camping. I asked them to move it to the other side of their car so it wouldn't be so loud. The other side of me there was a huge family with kids running around everywhere. I felt like there were too many people surrounding me. I was used to camping in the middle of nowhere with nobody around. It was Friday night so I was sure it would be worse the next day. There would be a ton of jet skis and boats on the lake, so it was probably good that we got here on a Friday when it wasn't as busy. Don't get me wrong, I LOVE it when people are outside enjoying nature. I just wasn't used to being around so many people for the last 10 weeks!

Chapter 22: Utah

We got rinsed off in the RV and then we took a walk on the beach and saw the beautiful sunset. It was breathtaking over the red rocks reflecting on the lake. It was the last one of our trip, and it didn't disappoint.

It was still really warm and a nice night for a walk, but the mosquitoes were attacking me big time, so I ran to the RV and we stayed there for the night! The sky was littered with stars. They were so pretty. I could have just laid on my chair outside and stared at them if it wasn't for the darn mosquitoes. The only constellation that I can ever find is the Big Dipper, but that doesn't mean I don't enjoy looking at them. I was wondering why we hadn't been enjoying the stars every night and then I remembered that it rained almost every night that we were in Colorado and many of the other states.

Saturday, July 11 - *We woke up at 7 a.m. and left the campground. I am happy that I didn't get stuck in the sand. I learned from the beginning of the trip to not drive with a full water tank so I emptied all of my water tanks before I left the campground. It was a very sad drive home and very boring because we took the freeway the entire way. It was a shock when we got into California. The gas prices were sky high and there was traffic everywhere, not to mention everything was brown. Yep, we were getting close to home! I was reminded of the beauty that we saw on this journey and how many amazing people that we met and incredible experiences that we had. As I was driving, I thought, I could probably write a book about this trip and hopefully inspire others to travel and be adventurous!*

We arrived home on July 11th after traveling 10,013 miles. Ten seems to be our number! We were gone 10 weeks, traveled 10,000 miles and Jack is 10 years old!

We can't believe this journey has come to an end. It was life changing in so many ways. It was an adventure every step of the way, and when I look back, I feel like it was perfect. It was a journey Jack and I will never forget! Thanks so much for taking it with us!!

For the weeks that followed the journey, I had the worst separation anxiety ever. I loved being with my mom all day every day for the past 10 weeks. When mommy returned to work at the hospital, she had to hire someone to come and walk me because she had to put me in a crate. I was chewing up anything that she left out that was hers. It broke mommy's heart to see me so unhappy. Time heals all and within a few months, I was okay again. After all, mommy takes me to do fun stuff in San Diego, too. You can follow our adventures at LeashYourFitness.com / blog

A special THANKS!

I don't know where to start! I never would have thought in a million years that I would write a book! This book would NOT be possible without the cheerleading from my Mastermind Group, especially my coach, Kelli Corasanti. They pushed me to not only write it, but finish it. I want to thank them for their support on the book and on the journey as well. Many of my teaching stops were sponsored by them, and I really appreciated it. They were the first to hear of my adventure and never once told me it was a crazy idea. They raised the bar and inspired me to keep living my dream! Kelli, you are an angel and I really appreciate all that you do for me including editing my book!

A special thanks for everyone who sponsored our classes around the country. It was super fun visiting your facilities and meeting your members. My hope is that everyone realized that it's fun to workout with your dog!

Thank you to all of the amazing people that I met on our journey, I wish I could have included everyone. Meeting people makes traveling so much more fun so thank you for being nice to us!

A special THANKS!

I also want to thank Arden Moore for doing the final edit on my book and for the endless answers to all of my questions on book publishing. You are a good friend and I am so happy that you were part of my journey.

I want to thank all of my family and friends for their support on all of my ideas and endeavors and always having my back. Thanks for cheering me on and being a part of Jack's Journey USA in so many ways!

Jim Hahn has been by my side and a constant encourager for everything "Jack!" From THE day that I got Jack, to starting my business, taking the journey and now writing the book, I couldn't ask for a more patient and encouraging person by my side. Not only did he make Spirit look beautiful, he continues to encourage me to follow my dreams no matter what it takes. He is a very special person!

A special thanks to Naomi Hillery and Crystal Nelson who did a fantastic job of running Leash Your Fitness while I was gone. They did such a great job, I seriously didn't think that I needed to return. I couldn't have done this journey without them "holding down the fort."

Thanks to my supervisor, Joe Freitas at UCSD, for allowing me to take 10 weeks off of work. He was right. People need vacations, and I had a whole new outlook when I returned! Smart Guy!

Thanks to all of my sponsors, ISLE, KIND Snacks, Kurgo, One Dog Organic Bakery and Sun Warrior Protein Powder for believing in Jack's Journey USA and helping me out with product and support.

Thanks to my parents, Norma and Jack Celapino. They were with me the entire way in Spirit, leading me to safety and to incredible things. It was reassuring having them on the journey with us. Thanks for my sense of adventure, Dad, and my independence, Mom! I love and miss you both!

And most important of all, I want to thank JACK! He is my best friend and he inspires me daily to do nice things for him and for other people and to get out and have fun! I love him with all of my heart, and I can't imagine my life without him!

Thanks for traveling with us!

Now it is YOUR turn!

Additional information

Gas: We spent $3,392 on gas. Two apps that we would recommend are: Gas Buddy and Costco. Sometimes, we saved 50 cents a gallon by going to Costco, so it is worth going out of your way a little if there is one nearby.

Camping: We spent $911 on camping and the average price per site was $27. We stayed at a lot of free places on our trip: friends and family, truck stops, parking lots, national forests and when we did camp, we mostly stayed at state parks, not RV parks, which are more expensive.

Food: I never ate at a fast food restaurant on my entire trip and only stopped at Starbucks twice and once was for my free birthday drink! I only ate at restaurants a few times when visiting friends and they were also nice enough to cook for me. I prepared all of my food and to be honest, I ate a lot of KIND snack bars.

For tips on camping with your dog, please go to www. LeashYourFitness.com and download your free .pdf.

Support our Sponsors

Kurgo Dog Supplies: www.Kurgo.com enter JACK20 road for 20% off your order

ISLE SUP: www.islesurfandsup.com enter Leash75 to get $75. Off your SUP

KIND Snacks: http://www.kindsnacks.com for healthy bars and snacks for your journey

SunWarrior Protein: https://sunwarrior.com/ for yummy smoothies

One Dog Organic unfortunately is no longer is business.

Camping Resources

BoondockersWelcome.com: A membership site where other campers will host you at their place of residence for free.

Days End: A membership site that has low cost or free places to stay all over the country. They also have a listing of what is near each stop.

Escapees.com: A membership site for support, discounts on RV parks, and a lot more.

GoPetFriendly.com: A free blog site that has tons of information on where to go with your dog.

Good Sam: A membership site that offers discounts on camping, gas, Camping World store purchases and other requirements for camping.

Roadtrippers.com: A free map system. Type in where you want to go and it will guide you to what is in the area.

Microsoft Streets and Maps: Program that you can purchase that doesn't require Internet. You can put in your destinations and it shows you the distance, what is around the area, routes to take, etc.

ReserveAmerica.com: largest provider of campsite reservations in North America.

Wheelingit.us: Great blog about full time RVing, camp information and much more!

If you are interested in knowing about any of the campgrounds that we stayed at, please visit <u>JacksJourneyUSA.com</u>, I put links to all of the campgrounds with the site numbers on each corresponding blog. I take a lot of time finding the perfect site at each spot, and I am happy to share that information with you to save you time and make your stay more enjoyable. Plus you can check out our cool photos!

About the Author

Dawn Celapino is Jack's mom and the owner of Leash Your Fitness. She loves everything outdoors including camping. Her and Jack have been in 34 states together. They enjoy hiking, trail running, kayaking, SUPing, Surfing, Working Out, Doing Yoga and just about anything as long as they are together. They are a team and have been featured in many National Magazines, TV shows, News Shows and Newspapers including Animal Planet, The Wall Street Journal and CNN. Jack's Journey USA is her first book.

For speaking engagements or media inquires contact Dawn at Dawn@LeashYourFitness.com

Follow Jack's adventures & other fun stuff at:
http://www.leashyourfitness.com/blog/
https://www.facebook.com/leashyourfitness
https://www.instagram.com/leashyourfitness/

38347101R00141

Made in the USA
Middletown, DE
18 December 2016